Prelude to Revolution

D1560081

PRELUDE to REVOLUTION

The Salem Gunpowder Raid of 1775

PETER CHARLES HOFFER

The Johns Hopkins University Press | *Baltimore*

Printed in the United States of America on acid-free paper

9 8 7 6 5 4 3 2 1

The Johns Hopkins University Press
2715 North Charles Street
Baltimore, Maryland 21218-4363
www.press.jhu.edu

Library of Congress Cataloging-in-Publication Data

Hoffer, Peter Charles, 1944–
    Prelude to revolution : the Salem gunpowder raid of 1775 / Peter Charles Hoffer.
      p. cm. — (Witness to history)
    Includes bibliographical references and index.
    ISBN-13: 978-1-4214-1005-0 (hardcover : acid-free paper)
    ISBN-10: 1-4214-1005-2 (hardcover : acid-free paper)
    ISBN-13: 978-1-4214-1006-7 (paperback : acid-free paper)
    ISBN-10: 1-4214-1006-0 (paperback : acid-free paper)
    ISBN-13: 978-1-4214-1007-4 (electronic)
    ISBN-10: 1-4214-1007-9 (electronic)
    1. Salem (Mass.)—History, Military—18th century. 2. Salem (Mass.)—History—
Colonial period, ca. 1600–1775. 3. Gunpowder—Political aspects—Massachusetts—
Salem—History—18th century. 4. Great Britain. Army—History—18th century.
5. Raids (Military science)—History—18th century. 6. Civil-military relations—
Massachusetts—Salem—History—18th century. 7. Colonists—Massachusetts—
Salem—History—18th century. 8. Massachusetts—History—Colonial period, ca.
1600–1775. 9. United States—History—Revolution, 1775–1783—Causes. 10. Collective
memory—United States—Case studies. I. Title.
    F74.S1H64 2013
    974.4′5—dc23   2013004818

A catalog record for this book is available from the British Library.

*Special discounts are available for bulk purchases of this book. For more information,
please contact Special Sales at 410-516-6936 or specialsales@press.jhu.edu.*

The Johns Hopkins University Press uses environmentally friendly book materials,
including recycled text paper that is composed of at least 30 percent post-consumer
waste, whenever possible.

CONTENTS

PREFACE

AFTER NEARLY 250 YEARS OF STUDY, Americans have still not come to a full understanding of the events that turned a sprawling patchwork of British North American colonies into one independent nation—and that is not a bad thing. After all, insofar as the American Revolution remains the most important event in our history, it makes sense that students of the past still ask basic questions about those events. What was the American Revolution? What did it change? Was it merely the beginning of a new nation? Or did it turn the world upside down, a true social upheaval? Who made it—a radical cadre? A mobilized common people? What caused it—a series of escalating misperceptions? The rise of a new idea of self-government? When did it begin—with the first years of colonization? With the imposition of new British designs upon American liberty after the French and Indian War? Or in the Pennsylvania Assembly building on a sultry, early July morning in 1776?

Historians know that some of the most important questions they have to ask are, "where does my story start?" and "when does my story end?" The following pages add what hopefully is an original contribution to the first of these inquiries about the American Revolution. The book relocates the beginning of the Revolution from its most popular conventional locations— the Freedom Trail in Boston, the House of Burgesses in Williamsburg, Independence Hall in Philadelphia, and the "rude bridge that spanned the flood" in Concord, Massachusetts—to an encounter at a raised drawbridge on the North River in Salem, Massachusetts. There a glimmer of independence, based on a new and revolutionary political and legal order, appeared to both sides in the controversy.

I believe the part of the story of the coming of the Revolution that has been slighted of late, a part that English historians fully recognize, is the part that the royal armed forces played in it. For only when the Regulars conceded defeat did a rebellion become the Revolution. The first time that happened was in Salem on February 26, 1775. That is the story I propose to tell in the following pages.

Prelude to Revolution

Prologue

ON A WINTER AFTERNOON in Salem, Massachusetts, across one hundred yards of dark, cold river, two resolute groups of men glared at one another. One leaf of the drawbridge that spanned the river was drawn up, and on the chain holding it aloft a ragged band of workmen, farm boys, sailors, and militia sat, hurling insults and incitements across the water. On the near shore, nearly three hundred British Regulars had massed in a formation meant to concentrate fire, but they had not leveled their weapons. They were awaiting their colonel's orders to begin the ritual of loading and firing. Colonel Alexander Leslie's mission was to cross the river and search for cannons and cannon carriages on the far side, and he was losing his patience as the sun set. Far from reinforcements and surrounded by townsmen warning him that he might start a fight he could not finish, he knew his options were narrowing. The American Revolution might have begun here, in Salem, on February 26, 1775. In one very important sense, it did. That beginning was not written in the blood of the Regulars or the patriots. It showed itself in Colonel Alexander Leslie's decision to negotiate a face-saving retreat.

This was not the first powder alarm in the winter of 1774/1775. British troops raided colonial powder magazines for months before the Salem raid. Nor was it the first time that colonists offered armed resistance to the British Regulars. It was, however, the first time that the British Army formally, in the person of a serving field commander, accepted the ignominy of voluntary withdrawal from a contested field. It was the first time that an assemblage of colonists (not an armed band or a military formation) cowed the British Regulars into formal negotiations, followed by a retreat from the field.

John Adams is credited with the now much-admired judgment that the Revolution did not begin with the Declaration of Independence or with the hostilities that accompanied it. He argued that the Revolution began in the minds and hearts of the people before July 4, 1776. That is surely true. What Adams omitted was how British arms factored into that change of hearts and minds. In fact, British armed forces played as central a role throughout the crisis that led to hostilities as they did during the war. For by 1774, the Regulars were visible symbol of crown sovereignty. So long as the Regulars contested the battlefield, the Revolution was not over.

If one adds the role of the Regulars to the story, as one should, one has to recalculate when and where the Revolution began. It could not have commenced with the plotting of Bostonian Samuel Adams's Sons of Liberty in 1765 or with the bluster of Virginia's Patrick Henry in 1774, for these did not involve a confrontation with British arms, much less the regular army's tacit admission of the effectiveness of resistance. This recalculation would seem to lead us to the shots fired at Lexington Green and in the town center of Concord, Massachusetts, but the retreat of the light infantry from the Concord raid was not the first time that the British had conceded the field to the armed citizenry of Massachusetts.

That came in Salem, nearly seven weeks previously. In 1856, an elderly Salem ship captain, retired from the East India trade, regaled the newly established Essex Institute with an account of a British powder raid on February 26, 1775. Of it, Charles Moses Endicott declared, "Here . . . we claim the first blow was struck in the war of independence by open resistance to both the civil and military power of the mother country." No blood was shed, but a significant change had taken place. An aroused civilian force, armed and determined to protect its rights, caused a British regiment to negotiate a retreat. The news of the Salem men's triumph spread far and wide. A squib in the *Gentleman's Magazine* for April 17, 1775, agreed: "It is reported that the Americans have hoisted their standard of liberty in Salem." Endicott was right. The Revolution began in Salem.[1]

Endicott understood that a Revolution in the hearts and minds of the people required a highly visible event, a ritual of the passing of legitimate power from an imperial sovereign to a sovereign people that everyone understood. Such a passing would not involve mere theory, but practice; not words on a page or read aloud, but evidence of self-government in action. One would then say that the American Revolution took place where Americans actually saw it, in the triumph of a resolute citizenry and the acquiescence of equally visible British military authority.

Such rituals are often part of the transference of power, whether the coronation and anointing of kings or the inauguration of presidents. Such rituals in the passing of power make it legitimate in the eyes of the people. Much as such a people might say they venerate a constitution of laws, of words on parchment or in statute books, without the public spectacle the laws lose their credence. No agency more clearly embodied the authority of the empire in its American provinces during the crisis period than the British Army and the Royal Navy. The Revolution began when Americans could envision the withdrawal of British armed might. When the minutemen at Concord drove the British out of the town, the British officers realized that American militia would not only refuse to cower before British arms, but also that they could defeat regular troops in pitched battle. When the Hessians at Trenton surrendered to General George Washington in 1776, it proved that the newly organized Continental Army could defeat European professional soldiers. When General John Burgoyne surrendered at Saratoga in 1777, the French realized that their hated British rivals might be humbled by the American colonists and agreed to a mutual defense treaty. At Yorktown in 1781, Lord Cornwallis's surrender (at which his bandsmen are reputed to have played "The World Turned Upside Down") led to the fall of Lord North's government in England and the beginning of peace negotiations.

But these were not the first of their kind, nor were British defeats in themselves withdrawals of British claims to authority. Instead, the first incidence of the gathering of a republican citizenry asserting the right to self-government of their own land and the unforced recession of British might came in Salem, on Sunday, February 26, 1775.

Return then to Salem, Massachusetts, a prosperous port city, on that Sunday afternoon on a cold and overcast New England coastal winter day, to follow a column of British Regulars as they disembark from longboats at a cove near the mouth of Marblehead Bay and march through farmland and pasture to Salem to seize cannons and powder housed at a local foundry. They find instead a raised drawbridge and an aroused citizenry, and, as Endicott told his townsmen, a Revolution began.[2]

One might rejoin that nothing happened at Salem—no one died, no one raised the flag of rebellion, no one penned new laws for a new nation. The tale of "Colonel Leslie's Retreat" that Salem men told to one another in an ever-widening spiral of detail and delight was much about nothing, like the satirical verse common in eighteenth-century English and colonial nursery rhymes: "Oh, the grand old Duke of York, / He had ten thousand men; / He marched them up to the top of the hill, / And he marched them down again." Apparently, historians have taken this view to heart.

After looking at the evidence for a long time, locating it in the longer story of colonial resistance to the Coercive Acts and the even longer story of the years after the French and Indian War, one should conclude that the gunpowder raid brought together a new world of popular politics and an old world of imperial British authority. Massachusetts men and women announced by word and demonstrated by deed that they were no longer subjects of the crown. Instead, they were citizens of a new kind of polity, one in which the people ruled themselves. By retreating, Colonel Alexander Leslie conceded the day to that new world.[3]

As word of his decision spread among the many groups of minutemen converging on Salem to dispute his mission, the glimmer of American glory grew to a flame. Might a show of even greater unity and determination not deter all British arms? It was Leslie's retreat—seen as a triumph of manly virtue and self-empowerment over corrupt and arrogant British might— that provided a key model for how Massachusetts's patriots would respond to General Thomas Gage's next military adventure. When Paul Revere and his crew of watchers saw the British under Gage's command sallying out of Boston on the night of April 18th, Leslie's retreat was surely somewhere near the front of their thinking. After all, this was another gunpowder raid. Rouse the countryside, bring out far more men and arms than had mustered on the North River a month and a half previously, and surely the British would also take Leslie's example to heart. That events did not turn out as the patriot leadership expected could hardly have been predicted. For the British garrison in Boston and the troops on Castle Island also knew about Leslie's retreat, and they were determined not to allow British arms to demonstrate such reticence again. They would teach the colonists a lesson. What began at Lexington was not the first scene of the first act of the Revolution, but scene two, and it would not have turned out as it did had both sides not read the lesson of Leslie's retreat in profoundly differing ways.

Chapter one of the present account introduces readers to Salem and its people. Although the town had prospered, personal and ideological differences during the crisis divided the elite and empowered the common folk. Chapter two focuses on the British armed forces' presence in the Massachusetts Bay Colony, and it follows the trail of two officers as they carried out an espionage mission for General Gage on the eve of the Salem raid. Their journal can be read as a travelogue, with views of a colony on the verge of independence. Chapter three tells the story of the raid and Leslie's retreat. Chapter four recovers and weighs the immediate impact of the raid on the thinking of British and American military leaders, along with its effect on the battles at Lexington and Concord three weeks later. Chapter five recalls the ways in which the memory of the raid was celebrated and then almost forgotten.

The Most Loyal Town in the Province

IN 1763, THERE WERE NO LOYALISTS in the American colonies—or, to be more accurate, British Americans were loyal to the empire. They gloried in its might and its recent conquest of its long-time enemies: the French, the Spanish, and their Indian allies. There were controversies over western lands, rumors of new measures to collect customs duties and taxes, and other potential trouble spots between the colonists and the incoming ministry of George Grenville, but in general there was no division between a protest party and a loyal party.

The town of Salem's part in the empire went almost as far back as the empire itself. In 1628 a small party of Puritans, radical English Protestant reformers, led by John Endicott, arrived at the little settlement of fishermen and Indians called Naumkeag on the rugged, rock-lined coast; renamed it Salem; and awaited the arrival of a great migration of fellow worshipers. The "hot-blooded Puritans" had tried for three generations to rid the Church of England of its impurities, and now many fled from royal persecution. They did not separate themselves from the Church of England, like their Pilgrim neighbors in Plimouth Plantation to the south of Salem. Instead, they wanted to erect a "cittie on a hill," in the words of Massachusetts Bay Company governor John Winthrop, so that all in England might see how true Christians established churches and worshiped.[1]

Without the Anglo-American imperial venture begun a half century earlier at Roanoke and promoted as part of the struggle against Britain's Roman Catholic Spanish foe, there would have been no haven in New England for the Puritans. The name New England itself was the coinage of one of the stalwart combatants in that Atlantic struggle against Spain, John Smith. Refused reentry to the Virginia colony at Jamestown, whose survival he had helped ensure, Smith, traveling with a whaling fleet, found himself sailing past the coastal home of the Massachusetts Indians in 1614. From that experience he wrote *A Description of New England* (1616), depicting the promise of settlement in glowing terms: "overgrown with all sorts of excellent good woods for building houses, bak[e]rs, boats, and ships, with an incredible abundance of most sorts of fish, much fowl, and sundry sorts of good fruits for man's use."[2]

But Salem under Endicott hardly fit Smith's prophecy of abundance and ease. The village was so disarrayed by starvation and disease in 1630 that Winthrop and the Puritans journeying with him to Massachusetts elected to bypass Salem for the Agawam Peninsula farther south. That settlement, named Boston after a town in northeastern England, would become the capital of the most populous Puritan refuge in North America, but Salem was not abandoned. To it came a young and intensely pious minister named Roger Williams. (Actually, he stopped in Boston first and decided not to serve its church.) In Salem he preached that the Church of England was too far gone in its corruption to be saved, even by the pious founders of Massachusetts. They must separate from it. In the coming years he would also preach that magistrates might not oppress the consciences of any man, for no one knew who was truly saved and who was a pious hypocrite. Driven from Massachusetts, Williams found his way to Narragansett Bay, where his little settlement of Providence Plantation later joined with other religious dissenters' settlements and became the colony of Rhode Island. It was the first of all the British possessions to legislate a limited form of religious freedom.[3]

While not entirely shedding its Puritan origins, seventeenth-century Salem was the beneficiary of English imperial trade, a port of call on the Atlantic highway that bound the British Isles to the slave coast of Africa, the West Indies, and the more southerly mainland colonies. Although the Salem shipowners and captains did not always obey the mercantilist policies that governed trade in the empire (as they were not above smuggling in goods from England's commercial rivals, the Dutch and the French), Salem's economic and physical growth mirrored that of the British Empire. Everyone did not prosper to an equal degree. As some grew wealthy, others—many others—were left behind. Every successful merchant's and ship captain's wealth rested on the labor of squadrons of dockworkers and day laborers, sailors, and ship builders. As leading families amassed land in the interior, western part of the town, ordinary farmers found they could give only smaller and smaller parcels to their children. A generation of landless men and women had appeared by the end of the seventeenth century.[4]

The coming of King William's War in 1689 made life for these young people even more perilous. The sea, never a safe place for fishermen, became even more dangerous, and the borderlands between New England and French Canada and Arcadia became the scene of horrific raiding. The refugees from villages along the coast of Maine, then a part of Massachusetts, flowed into Salem, bringing with them stories of pitiless, red-painted Indian warriors and their demonic French Jesuit masters. Dysentery stalked the land. It seemed as if Satan himself had targeted Salem. Certainly fear of the Devil had. Every textbook in American history tells some variant of this story: in the winter of 1691/1692, the entire community of Salem was wracked with terror. An ugly combination of political uncertainty, widespread religious fanaticism, and deeply held superstition tore at the ties that bound the community together. A settled politics at home might have quelled the panic, but Massachusetts was temporarily without a charter of government, awaiting the pleasure of the new rulers of England, William III and Mary. The tangled web of mistrust and animosity reached its climax in a rural village in the far western corner of Salem, later incorporated by the General Court (the lower house of assembly) of the colony as the town of Danvers. Some in the village had wanted to retain the services of minister Samuel Parris. Others had wanted him and his family to depart. Quarrels over the retention of ministers were common in New England towns, but this one was carried on with great venom because it overlaid a struggle between two powerful families, the Putnams supporting Parris and the Proctors undermining him.[5]

To this was added the sudden, inexplicable illness of Parris's nine-year-old daughter, Betsy or Betty (the name is recorded both ways), and his eleven-year-old niece, Abigail, a servant living with Parris in the parsonage. They began to experience seizures, which the local doctor could not diagnose.

Whatever the cause of their malady, it soon spread to other girls in the village. Adults were baffled and fearful until the girls accused three local women, one of them Parris's slave Tituba, of being witches.

The men and women of early-modern New England believed that the Devil could give supernatural powers to women and men: the power to travel in spectral form, and the ability to harm the Devil's enemies. Tituba confessed that a "man in black" had forced her to sign a book, and her confession, ironically, saved her life. She (along with others who confessed to being witches) survived the noose. In the meantime, the prodding of parents and ministers had refocused what might have been a combination of preadolescent anxiety and playacting into accusations of a capital crime. Frightened by the hideous shapes of their own imaginings, the parents and preachers turned to the magistrates to scourge the witches and their Satanic master from the land. Pretrial hearings, over which Salem magistrates John Corwin and John Hathorne presided, turned on the performances of the allegedly afflicted girls, who exclaimed in chorus that each suspect was assaulting them in a form invisible to all but the witches' caterwauling victims.

On May 14, 1692, the newly appointed governor, William Phipps, returned from England to find the jails overflowing with suspected witches. Faced with the crisis, he used his discretion to fashion a special court to hear and decide the cases. It met in Salem's town hall. William Stoughton, the lieutenant governor, was the chief judge, and he determined to root out the witches. That meant allowing spectral evidence that only the alleged victims could see. Trial juries, browbeaten by Stoughton and shocked by the ensemble performance of the girls, convicted all the defendants brought to trial between June 5th and September 21st. The trials were swift affairs, life and death determined in a few hours. Defendants were tried in groups. Thirteen women and five men were carted to Gallows Hill above the North River and there hanged for the crime of witchcraft. One old man, Giles Corey, was pressed to death with heavy stones for refusing to accede to the authority of the court by pleading to the charges. By the end of September 1692, nearly two hundred more suspects were in jail awaiting their turn at trial. Four of the suspects had died in jail and many more were sick. Those who were first accused lived in or near the village, but by late spring the girls' accusations were boldly reaching out to leading members of the port community. No one was safe.

Headed by Boston's Samuel Willard, the leading ministers (except for Boston's Cotton Mather, who approved of the conduct of the trials, and old

John Higginson of Salem, who did not know what to believe) came to regard the proceedings as fundamentally flawed. They convinced minister Increase Mather, Cotton's father and the leader of the colony's ministerial association, to turn their criticism into a tract on the dangers of believing spectral evidence. He argued for the priority of religious laws over civil ordinances. Spectral visitations might be the Devil's instrument to fool the credulous and cast blame on the innocent. Thus permitting spectral evidence in court was playing the Devil's game. Increase Mather's work was widely circulated. Phipps was convinced and ordered a stop to the trials. They would reconvene in the winter, but this time spectral evidence was not allowed. All but three women were acquitted at this new round of trials, and Phipps pardoned them as well as everyone else. The General Court provided a modest subsidy for the families of the executed men and women and, in 1711, passed a resolution clearing their names. Witchcraft accusations recurred in Salem, but never again did the colonial court take them seriously. The invisible world in which specters of witches danced around fires in the forest depths and flew to meetings with the Devil retained its fascination in Salem's popular culture, but ministers and magistrates refused to participate in any more witch hunts. The judgment of later Salem chroniclers was that "the 'afflicted' children" had simply "gone too far." In any case, Salem was victimized by a "general conspiracy" among the historians of Boston and the other New England towns that prosecuted witches, "trying to fasten the whole responsibility and disgrace of the witchcraft prosecutions upon Salem."[6]

By all accounts, by the beginning of the new century Salem was determined to put the scandal behind it and get on with business as usual. The scene of that business was the town's streets. The front rooms of merchants' homes doubled as offices. Craftsmen's workshops opened onto the streets. Retailers and repairmen advertised their wares and services in street-front windows and with signs that projected above the street. Like many of New England's towns, including its great commercial rivals Boston and Newport, Rhode Island, eighteenth-century Salem had grown beyond the original street layout in unplanned ways. "New" streets, as yet unnamed because no householders of note had built there, ran along both sides of the North River and on the other side of Salem Neck, along the wharves. Salem's street plan resembled that of the English villages from which the first settlers came, with streets changing their direction and names, crossing one another at acute and oblique angles, and varying in width from alley to avenue and back again.

Paved with cobblestones, the main streets were noisy and smelly—the carts and wagons had iron-rimmed wheels that groaned and whined, and the sanitation squad of local pigs squealed and snorted. All manner of rich and poor lived next to one another, though everyone knew that John Derby, the tailor whose shop lay at the corner of Main Street (later Essex Street) and St. Peter's Lane was not the same "quality" as John Derby, the son of Richard Derby Sr., whose lands and wharf were the most extensive in town. The early eighteenth-century city featured the rich and poor living cheek by jowl, but by the eighteenth century's midpoint, the dark and brooding two-and-one-half-story, boxlike houses of the Corwins and the Hathornes in the west end of Salem were giving way to the elegant, symmetrical Georgian homes of the shipowners and overseas merchants. In these Georgian town homes, casement windows were out of fashion, and double-hung sash windows were all the rage; the result was airier, brighter interiors.

Homes not only symbolized refinement, they announced the owners' status. The Crowninshields, for example, visually boasted of their market success with an elegant clapboard two-and-a-half-story Georgian mansion on Essex Street. Not to be outdone, Richard Derby Sr., whose fleet of thirteen fishing vessels docked at his own Salem wharf on Derby Street, married his son, Elias Hacket, into the Crowninshield clan and ordered construction of a red-brick town home on Derby Street for the couple.

As bustling as mid-eighteenth-century Salem might be, its history was not forgotten. It was still surrounded by open fields. Across the North River, on the hill above the foundry in what were known as the North Fields, one could still imagine the suspected witches mounting the scaffolds on Gallows Hill. Along the portion of the South River called the Mill Pond (in 1693 the town dammed the river to allow the Malloon family to build a gristmill), the South Fields stretched on both sides of the road to Marblehead. (In Marblehead the road was called the Country Road.) Real estate development was remaking the edges of these open spaces. After the Revolutionary War the Marblehead Highway, renamed in honor of the Marquis De Lafayette, would become an elegant enclave of the well-to-do. It was an early example of the favored-quarter district of nineteenth-century American cities.[7]

By mid-eighteenth century, Salem Harbor's growing number of wharves provided safety from the North Atlantic gales. Though rarely more than twenty-five feet in depth, the harbor was sufficiently deep to welcome the merchant vessels that plied the Atlantic Rim sea routes. These connected

Salem, and the produce of its farmers and fishermen, to the English West Indian sugar islands. Derby and the other shipowners' wharves jutted out into the harbor, each with its own warehouses and storerooms. The wharves allowed the ships to unload cargos without going aground. Derby's own long wharf jutted 800 feet out into the harbor.[8]

As part of the growing British Empire, and because of the advantages that shippers had within the empire, Salem's resident population doubled: from a few thousand men and women in 1700 to nearly six thousand souls by 1770. Many of these were the fourth and fifth generations of townspeople, making Salem one of the most "adhesive" of the New England towns. But unlike other adhesive towns such as Andover, eighteenth-century Salem had become a port of origin; a school for sailors, pilots, and ship captains; and a factory for ship making and ship repair. Indeed, Salem was so tied to the sea that by the end of the French and Indian War in 1763, few of the townspeople made their living working the land.[9]

This last great war for empire in North America had been good to Salem. "Trade flourishes at Salem," Samuel Gardner wrote in his diary in 1759, this not despite, but because of the war. Salem men owned over 10 percent of the colony's fishing fleet, and the flagships of that fleet, two-masted schooners, brought their cod down from the Newfoundland Banks to the town's wharves. After 1759 the French threat to the fishing fleets had abated, and the demand for cod exceeded its prewar level. The Royal Navy protected Salem shipping to the far outposts of empire, a fact that merchants well knew. The " 'Charming Pollys,' and 'Pattys,' and 'Nancys' "—Salem shipowners' most popular names for their vessels—plied the Atlantic, though the risks of cargo loss by storm, misadventure, and enemy action never left the merchants' minds.[10]

But by the war's end in 1763, Salem was once again ready to grow rich on the spoils and the benefits of empire. Its ships and its merchants took part in the lucrative slave-and-supplies trade to the British sugar islands in the Caribbean. The consumer rage for durable trade goods resumed. From Salem these imports traveled over roads to the interior, appearing in farmers' homes and village shops. The connection to empire had brought the city and its leaders wealth and status, and there was little reason to assume that the benefits of empire would not multiply in the coming years.[11]

Salem society mirrored the diversity of the post-war empire. Three congregational churches vied with a Society of Friends and the Anglican St. Peter's

Salem Harbor, ca. 1771. Courtesy of the John Carter Brown Library at Brown University.

for congregants. Four hundred and fifty houses, including commercial establishments, catered to locals and a mixed bag of transients from all over the Atlantic. Free and slave Africans, Portuguese and Spanish sailors, the occasional French-speaking trader, as well as people from throughout the British Isles frequented the inns and taverns near the docks. Not quite as polygot a population as New York City or Philadelphia, Salem's was nevertheless a far cry from its Puritan origins.[12]

The imperial wars had wrought a subtle but profound change in the upper reaches of Salem society. Land ownership, which was the basis of early fortunes, could not compete with mercantile wealth. Although they still had lovely homes along Main Street in Salem and their family names gave them access to the front pews in the meetinghouses, some of the midcentury leaders, like Samuel Browne, were not able to pass their economic leadership on to their offspring. William Browne, his in-law Benjamin Lynde, and their circle—once the most wealthy families in the town, based on extensive land and commercial holdings—now depended more on rents and official patronage.[13]

Old wealth and esteem still gained political office, creating friction between the Brownes and Lyndes and the newer rich, such as the Derby family. To retain their status, "provincial lawyers," like Browne, "courted official favor at every level," from crown patronage to the local electorate. While others, such as the Derbys, also aspired to local office, higher office was still beyond their grasp. New wealth or old, the town expected its elite to perform the duties of political leadership, a deference system that was true for most eastern-seaboard New England towns.

William Browne was still a man of parts, much respected by his propertied townsmen. After service in the French and Indian War, he was chosen colonel of the Essex County militia by his men and elected as the town's representative to the sitting of the General Court, still the lower house of assembly. Born and educated in Salem and at Harvard, a lawyer and large landholder, Browne was a man of conservative tastes and politics. He was the customs collector for the ports of Salem and Marblehead, but he was relieved of his duties in 1767 for alleged failure to rigorously perform them (whether through languor or an unwillingness to prosecute his fellow elite merchants, one cannot determine). Still, he, along with sixteen other Rescinders, sought royal favor by rejecting Samuel Adams's circular letter of 1768 (protesting the Townshend Duties), assuring the ministry of their loyalty after the Townshend Duties protest. For this Browne was appointed to the colonial Council (the upper legislative house) and to the Superior Court of Judicature. He was never again chosen by the freeholders to represent them, however. His reputation, in this increasingly divisive political atmosphere, was no longer secure from reproach, but when General Thomas Gage was named royal governor of the colony and arrived in Salem, Browne was one of his welcomers.[14]

Men with more recent wealth, such as Richard Derby Sr., did not defer to older elites like Browne, and the former found a way to undermine the political influence of the old elite in the protest movement of 1763. Browne and his clique could be made a target of the colonial Whigs' resentment. Indeed, the use of the term Whig by the opponents of parliamentary enactments that cribbed the colonists' economic and political autonomy implied that Browne was an enemy of the people, a Tory. Reused language like this recalled the turbulent English politics of the late seventeenth century, when self-styled Whigs defended parliamentary prerogative against King James II's supporters. (In that era "Tory" denoted an Irish bandit, but it has since been sanitized and now is the name of the British Conservative party.)

As the protests grew over Grenville's so-called reforms, including the enforcement of customs duties and the imposition of stamp taxes, the elite of Salem divided further. Older-family leaders like the Brownes, Benjamin

Lynde, the Pickman clan, Samuel Curwen, and others decided that their best interests lay in continued expressions of loyalty. Others, notably Richard Derby Sr. and Jr. and the Cabots, began to view the imperial connection differently. They quietly joined with the protesters. These Whigs were the authors of Salem's instructions of October 21, 1765, to the colonial assembly: "We the inhabitants of said Salem, being fully convinced that the act lately passed by the Parliament of Great Britain, commonly called the Stamp Act, would if carried into execution be excessively grievous and burthensome to the inhabitants of this his Majesty's loyal province."

It was a respectful petition of a type previously used many times by town freeholders to instruct their elected representatives. Moreover, Salem did not break out in the anti–Stamp Act protests, parades, burnings-in-effigy, and tarring-and-featherings that marked the "riotous temper" of protests in Boston, Newport, New York City, and other urban centers. Indeed, John Adams and other Whigs were concerned that Salem might not join in the protests at all. The "sentiments" of the signers, another boilerplate term common in these instructions, seemed measured. But the ill-will toward Parliament was growing among the Derbys and their cohort. "Public harmony" and good order could only be maintained if the Act was rescinded.

Thus when John Hathorne's ship appeared in the North River wharves the following January, self-styled Sons of Liberty met it and demanded to see if the ship bore the hated stamped paper. Among the mob were "respectable people," including two of the town's selectmen, and they hosted the burning of a jackboot (a reference to King George III's hated advisor, the Earl of Bute), after which the company retired to a local tavern to drink to the king's health.[15]

Each incident, each act of Parliament, each response by colonial protesters, made neutrality harder and harder for members of the elite, and made elite unity more and more difficult to maintain. Men like Browne and Derby were not natural enemies. They were businessmen who had cooperated in the past and shared the same personal values. Browne was not a believer in royal absolutism, and Derby was not a political or social radical. But the ground under them was shaking, and the gap between them widening.

The repeal of the Stamp Act in 1766 was followed not by peace, but by another seeming provocation: the passage of duties on tea, lead, and other imports, undertaken by Parliament at the urging of Charles Townshend, the chancellor of the exchequer. Townshend's death shortly after the new duties were imposed on colonial imports did not mitigate colonial anger. It was against this act that Whig pamphleteers, like John Dickinson of Pennsylvania, railed "No taxation without representation" in Parliament. In 1768, the General Court framed a petition to the crown against the duties, and when Lieutenant Governor Thomas Hutchinson refused to cooperate, a second vote, 92 to 17, refused to rescind the resolution. The seventeen who voted against the petition, including William Browne, became even more odious to the Whig party in the colony. When a Salem town meeting was called to censure Browne, his allies in the town protested against the protest. Signing the remonstrance were Francis Cabot, John Higginson, Thomas Barnard, Samuel Curwen, Joseph Bowditch, Benjamin Lynde, Benjamin Pickman, Andrew Oliver and, not surprisingly, Browne himself. As later events took shape, Barnard, Higginson, and Cabot would reconsider and become patriots. The others would remain loyal to the crown when the final crisis came.[16]

A war of words turned into street combat when the Whigs called for a non-importation agreement to force Parliament to reverse the new duties. Boston led the way, but Salem could hardly hide, given the importance of imports to its economy. The non-importation strategy was the centerpiece of resistance, circulated among other colonial legislatures by Samuel Adams in a precursor to the later activities of the Committees of Correspondence. Non-importation was never completely successful, but it kept passions roiled. The language of resistance had shifted from polite petition to angry remonstrance, lessons on liberty dictated by the selectmen for assemblymen Richard Derby Jr. and Timothy Pickering to deliver to the General Court: "A time when the situation of publick affairs calls for the greatest exertions of wisdom, prudence, integrity and firmness . . . it demands your closest attention to our true and real interests, and to those rights and privileges which we are justly entitled to."[17]

Gentlemen saw themselves as still writing to and for gentlemen—certainly not the murmurings of a discontented rabble—but something new and ominous had happened: the landing of regiments of British Regulars in Boston in a time of peace. What had been a civilian dispute over politics now took on a martial hue. Two years later, on March 5, 1770, when a crowd began to pelt the guardpost in front of the town's customhouse, a commotion followed and someone ordered the guard to fire on the mob (or one of the guards' muskets accidentally fired). The "Boston Massacre," as patriot protest-organizer Paul Revere called it, brought four civilians who had been holed up in the customhouse, eight soldiers, and their captain to trial for manslaughter. Benjamin Lynde of Salem presided, John Adams and Josiah Quincy Jr. (both avid patriots) defended the men, and the jury (hand-picked loyalists), acquitted all but two of them. Two soldiers were found guilty of involuntary manslaughter and branded on the thumb.

The merchants of Salem, though free of the irritant of occupying troops, voted to enforce non-importation agreements that Samuel Adams had proposed. But the lines were not yet so firmly drawn that a man of conscience, or a man who saw his interests shifting, might not cross them. John Adams, already a fiery patriot, did. As he recalled in his diary, three years later: "The Part I took in Defence of Cptn. Preston and the Soldiers, procured me Anxiety, and Obloquy enough. It was, however, one of the most gallant, generous, manly and disinterested Actions of my whole Life, and one of the best Pieces of Service I ever rendered my Country. Judgment of Death against those Soldiers would have been as foul a Stain upon this Country as the Executions of the Quakers or Witches, anciently. As the Evidence was, the Verdict of the Jury was exactly right."[18]

In the meantime, as Samuel Adams and the other leaders of the anti-Hutchinson agitation hoped, the demand for conformity with non-importation proved to be a continual irritant to imperial authorities and their loyalist allies. Adams banked on the regulatory officiousness of New England town councils. There was already a semidictatorial tradition among these bodies when it came to regulating the local economy. The Salem committee to inspect the warehouses and shops for British goods included Richard Derby Jr., Jonathan Ropes, and Colonel David Mason. It was not, as were some others of its type, "peopled largely by men with little of no previous political status," but missing were Browne and the other Rescinders.[19]

The committee claimed for itself the authority to publish the identities of the noncompliant. Merchants whose trade most depended on importations from England, such as Francis Higginson, found that their efforts at self-help (they allegedly broke into caches of sequestered imports to rescue their consignments) brought fines and confiscation from the committee. The town had no legal basis for the fines and confiscations, and when the importers brought the issue to court, they won damages from the committee, but the episode forced the fence-sitters to choose sides. Higginson shifted his allegiance to the Whigs. Pickering, who had vacillated, threw his lot in with Higginson. Others who appeared hesitant in their allegiance, such as Judge Nathaniel Ropes, were subject to physical and verbal abuse by the crowd.

For now the elite leadership of the protest was forced to share that role with lesser men: insurgents who linked personal grievances against loyalists with a larger sense of their own rightful empowerment—the "self-capacitating of the common people"—to turn the protest against Parliament to their own more egalitarian ends. To make non-importation work, the elite patriots had to mobilize ordinary men and women. Having set them on the course of protest, there was no stopping them—except, perhaps, with British shot and steel.[20]

Thomas Hutchinson, a cautious man whose ancestors had been among the founders of the colony and who had benefited greatly from royal patronage, was not entirely unsympathetic to the protests, but as lieutenant governor at the time of the Stamp Act protests, Hutchinson was one of the victims of mob violence and came to abhor the street politics of what was known as the popular party. He became governor of the province when Governor Francis Bernard abruptly decamped for England. Remembering how the mob had trashed his home, Hutchinson favored the deployment of troops in Boston but confined his opinions to private correspondence. When his letters fell into the hands of Whig Benjamin Franklin, who sent their contents back to Massachusetts, Hutchinson's position became untenable.[21]

Tone deaf to the rising clamor of colonial protests, Parliament passed the Tea Act of 1773. Innocuous on its face, it imposed a monopoly on colonial tea importers. Henceforth, they were required to buy from the East India Company. Tea was a luxury of the colonial diet that many colonists enjoyed, but Samuel Adams and his allies objected to the way in which British officialdom dictated to American palates and pocketbooks. When Boston importers refused to return their cargoes of tea to British ports, a band of hooligans left the Boston town meeting that Adams had called, assembled on the wharves, broke into the ships' cargo holds, and tossed the tea chests into the harbor. Parliament's response was a series of enactments closing the port of Boston and reorganizing the colonial government.

While the Port Act only affected Boston's harbor, leaving Salem and other Massachusetts ports untouched, its tone was severe and patronizing: "Whereas dangerous commotions and insurrections have been fomented and raised in the town of *Boston,* in the Province of *Massachusetts Bay,* in *New England,* by divers ill-affected persons, to the subversion of his Majesty's Government, and to the utter destruction of the public peace, and good order of the said town . . . it shall not be lawful for any person or persons whatsoever, to lade or put, or cause or procure to be laden or put, off or from any quay, wharf, or other place, within the said town of *Boston*." In short, the port of Boston was nailed shut. For the people of the town dependent on the port, the Act was an unmitigated disaster. It put them out of work and denied them the food and clothing that they imported. Patriot newspapers and pamphlets were soon debasing the Port Act as one of the Intolerable Acts.[22]

The second of these was the Massachusetts Government Act of 1774. Its key provision read "that from and after August 1, 1774, so much of the charter [of 1691] . . . which relates to the time and manner of electing the assistants or counsellors for the said province, be revoked, . . . and that, from and after the said August 1, 1774, the council, or court of assistants of the said province for the time being, shall be composed of such of the inhabitants or proprietors of lands within the same as shall be thereunto nominated and appointed by his Majesty." Americans today see constitutions as fundamental law, preceding and empowering all government, but the colonial charter was not a constitution of that sort at all. It did not confer rights on the colonists. The charter was simply a list of privileges the crown allowed the founders and later settlers in a colony, and it might be rescinded or altered as the crown saw fit.[23]

While the Port Act was, in effect, a criminal punishment applied to an entire town for the acts of a few who might or might not live in the town and might be decried as a departure from accepted criminal procedure, the Reorganization Act was well within the crown's legitimate authority. The terms of the charters were wholly at the discretion of the crown, for, in law, the colonies themselves were the personal possession of the monarch or his designates. Whatever degree of self-government existed in the colonies was a privilege that the crown could withdraw. The crown had already revised the charter of the Massachusetts Bay Colony twice, once in 1684 and once in 1692. The patriot leaders regarded the reorganization of the charter in a different light, however: as proof of a British plot to enslave the colonists by denying them old and established liberties. Whatever might have been the legal standing of the two acts in British imperial law, Lord North's ministry could not have played more perfectly into Samuel Adams's hands. The first fruits were the removal of Hutchinson from office. He sailed to England, carrying with him a letter of thanks from grateful loyalists, and died in the home country in 1780.[24]

Hutchinson's replacement was Lieutenant General Thomas Gage. Gage was not Lord North's first choice, but his superiors' need to know first-hand from him about the military situation in the colonies had brought Gage, commander of his majesty's forces in North America, back from his New York City headquarters to report to King George's advisors. Gage impressed the king with his knowledge and his bearing, in part because Gage came from the landed aristocracy himself. He had spent his entire adulthood in the army, rising from ensign to command rank, and could be trusted to be firm. Though not brilliant, he had served with calm competence in European and American theaters of war, never quite victorious but always avoiding blame for failure. He concluded his service in the French and Indian War as commander-in-chief of the royal forces in North America. His stint at army headquarters in the city of New York allowed him to witness the anti–Stamp Act riots there. His earlier reports on them showed a facile view of colonial politics. In 1766, he wrote the following to Lord Conway, his majesty's secretary of war: "After the many proofs his majesty has given of his paternal tenderness toward all his people . . . and the temper and moderation of the addresses shown in both houses [of parliament] . . . none but the most stubborn and factious spirits can refuse to submit the decision of their constitutional rights to the wisdom of the British legislature." He knew all about the danger that the empire faced from opponents of Parliament in the colonies, however, and during his sojourn at the royal court in 1773, he advised the king (according to a letter George III wrote to Lord North) that the people of Boston "will be lions, whilst we are lambs, but if we take the resolute part, they will be very meek." For that incautious boast, the impression he made on the king, and his availability, Lord North ordered Gage to return to Boston and enforce the Boston Port Act.[25]

Naming Gage as the governor of Massachusetts under the new charter also had precedent in earlier American history. Some of the crown appointees under various charters were titled governors-general. They were often senior officers in the British Army who regarded their colonial office as a kind of pension. Some, like William Hunter of New York, proved able administrators. Others, like Edmund Andros of New York and New England, were autocrats. These officers' duties included guarding the frontiers of the colony from imperial rivals and Indian enemies, ensuring the safe passage and settlement of immigrants to the frontiers, and other primarily military functions, though their salaries were not paid by the crown. Instead, colonial assemblies were to levy the colonists to pay for the governors, giving the local magnates sitting in the legislatures great leverage over the governors or their lieutenants (since some of the appointees remained in England and chose substitutes to travel to America and preside in their stead). But Gage represented an advance on this model—he was not there to enjoy his retirement from active service.[26]

Gage's arrival in Boston on May 13, 1774, aboard the port ship HMS *Lively*, was met with an almost shrill enthusiasm. The troops who accompanied him, some three thousand men, joined with those already bivouacked at the fortress on Castle Island, less than two miles to the southeast of Boston Harbor, and lined the wharf to formally acknowledge his assumption of civil authority. The turn-out and stand-to of the troops (line after line of bright red coats), the troops' huzza (an almost primitive cry of martial ardor), and the firing of weapons all presented the onlookers with proof that the British Empire was close by. Such visually significant symbolism could hardly be missed; its very intent was to overawe and impose submission. The salute was part of a military culture, of which the parade in honor of a commander was the mildest of expressions. More violent examples of this genre of ritual enabled killings on the field of battle.[27]

There was a brittle edge to the welcome that the military ceremony could not conceal, however. While the justices of the county court, like the men at arms, "at once testify to their loyalty of the King, and to pay your excellency their dutiful respects . . . we flatter ourselves that it will be acceptable to the people over whom you preside . . . and the happiness of British subjects," the Whigs were far from content with the change in government. The message was clear to the seamen, dockworkers, and other middling folk who watched quietly from the hillside above the quay: civil order now rested on royal arms. Once the embodiment of an almost spiritual attachment, now the imperial connection depended on the Regulars.[28]

The address that the loyalists of Salem presented to Gage on June 11th expressed their hopes for a reconciliation with the crown in terms that older generations would recognize—deference rather than submission, junior partners in a joint venture rather than obedient children or subjects of an arbitrary distant power. The language was hammered out from nearly a hundred years of debate over the meaning of the Glorious Revolution of 1688 in England, the language of rights that Parliament had imposed on the incoming monarchs William and Mary, and the ideals of a balanced government of mixed orders (people, aristocracy, crown) and ordered liberty: "We, merchants and others, inhabitants of the ancient town of Salem, beg leave to approach your Excellency with our most respectful congratulations on your arrival in this place. We are deeply sensible of his Majesty's paternal care and affection to this province, in the appointment of a person of your Excellency's experience, wisdom and moderation, in these troublesome and difficult times."

The address informed Gage that whatever might be happening in Boston or in the hinterlands, "we rejoice that this town is graciously distinguished for that spirit, loyalty, and reverence for the laws, which is equally our glory and happiness. From that public spirit and warm zeal to promote the general happiness of men, which mark the great and good, we are led to hope under your Excellency's administration for everything that may promote the peace, prosperity, and real welfare of this province." There was some sincerity in these words, for Salem had never been the scene of anti-crown violence, its streets filled with torch-bearing mobs or the homes of its customs officials torn down.

Salem's mercantile elite was sensible of the fact that the town's well-being depended on its overseas commerce, and that this, in turn, depended on the protection of the Royal Navy, good credit terms from English and Scottish brokers, and access to all the ports of call in the empire. "We beg leave to commend to your Excellency's patronage the trade and commerce of this place, which, from a full protection of the liberties, persons and properties of individuals, cannot but flourish." The address also invited Gage to shift the locus of government from Boston to Salem. There was nothing new in this; on occasion the General Court had met in Cambridge, across the Charles River from the capital. "And we assure your Excellency we will make it our constant endeavors by peace, good order, and a regard for the laws, as far as in us lies, to render your station and residence easy and happy."

The signers regarded themselves as the best men, and they hoped for peace and good will as much as for their own advantage. According to the social and political ideology in which they were raised, the best men should govern. These men had no title or claim by blood to rule, but their authority rested on "reputation, on opinion, on having one's claim to gentility accepted by the world." Such a reputation brought "respectability and credit," along with deference in official posts. They had little more to gain from Gage's favor then they had enjoyed before the crisis, but much to fear from a revolution that would put lesser men—"the harmless, ignorant multitude . . . wanton and bold, in pride of youth, deaf to remonstrance, blind to truth"—over them.[29]

The signers were both Whig and Tory, a who's who of Salem's finest. Not all would remain loyalists, and of those who did, some would return from exile during the war. Others had or would soon switch sides. Thomas Barnard, the son of a leading minister by the same name, had been a loyalist until hostilities erupted. He had signed the address to Governor Hutchinson in 1768, but later chose the patriot side. William Vans leaned to the loyalist side, in part because of his connections with the Pickmans and Samuel Curwen, but Vans, too, elected to remain in Salem as a patriot rather than flee as a loyalist. Curwen left Salem and returned in 1784 to live quietly (with a British pension for his troubles) until his death in 1799. Some of the families, like the Higginsons, the Cabots, and the Putnams, would carve out distinguished careers in the new nation.[30]

Gage saw Salem as a center of loyalty, but he put too much faith in the candor of the memorialists. Their words were hopeful rather than conclusory. Most of the town's leaders now understood that the civil ties holding the British North American empire together had frayed, along with the loyalty the patriots once owed to their distant rulers. Instead, the glue of empire was military force. As the town fathers of Wrentham, Massachusetts (a village a few miles away from the Rhode Island border), told their representatives to the General Court on June 3, 1774, Britain ruled the colony "by a fleet and army," reducing the colonists to a "conquered" people. Over and over in their various towns' instructions to their elected assemblymen, the selectmen decried the force of British arms arrayed against the protests.[31]

The scope of Gage's options to restore order were fast narrowing. He could rule by fiat, but that would effectually grant a kind of independence to those parts of the colony not under military occupation. While he would be enforcing the Port Act, the rest of his political task—to govern according to the revised charter—would be forfeit. Instead, he assayed a legal solution, calling for a new session of the General Court and hoping that he could somehow control its deliberations. He selected Salem for the meeting, instead of Boston, where radicals like Samuel Adams and Paul Revere were camped, because he was not so well-informed about what Salem's leaders were thinking. Perhaps his loyalist informants (like Browne) had reassured him when they should have warned him. He put Richard Derby Sr. on the council of the colony, when Derby was already a leader of the opposition party. Or perhaps

Gage identified himself with men like Derby, assuming (for the present correctly) that the Derbys, like the Brownes of the loyalist party, did not want to disrupt the benefits the empire conferred on Salem's economy.

While Gage was busy officially rejecting Boston's Solemn League and Covenant to resist the parliamentary acts, the council was assembling in the city. Under the old charter of 1692, the council was elected, subject to the royal governor's approval. Under the new charter, whose text arrived in May, the governor summoned a council of his own choosing. This was the same system that existed in most of the colonies (Rhode Island and Connecticut excepted), but Massachusetts's patriot faction protested again. So Gage adjourned the elected council and resolved to have the entire General Court meet on June 1st in Salem.

As had happened in his arrival in Boston, when he traveled to Salem on June 2nd, Gage mistook ceremony for sincerity. He stayed at William Browne's house, then shifted his headquarters to Danvers, previously called Salem Village. Whether or not he knew that it was the cockpit of the Salem witchcraft accusations and hearings, he did not entertain there. The loyalists of Salem visited one another, however, their spirits buoyed by his presence. They thanked him in the *Essex Gazette* of June 14th; the 48 signers included the Cabots, Benjamin Lynde, the Pickmans, and Samuel Curwen. The patriots also addressed him in respectful terms: "We are deeply affected with the sense of our public calamities . . . and we hope your excellency will use your endeavors to prevent a fu[r]ther accumulation of evils on [Boston's] already sorely distressed people." By now, their signatories were as predictable as those of the loyalists: Timothy Pickering, Richard Derby Jr., and David Mason, among others. William Browne signed the address as well, hoping that the die was not cast.[32]

Although the grievance against British policy was directed at the occupying forces, military service past and present was an asset for patriot leaders. Colonel David Mason, for example, was an artisan who, despite little more than a grade-school education, became a devotee of Benjamin Franklin's experiments with electricity. Mason supplemented his income by giving lectures on the new science. He was also a student of the physics of artillery, and during the French and Indian War he served first as an officer in the colonial militia, then as a captain in a British artillery unit. He had the misfortune of seeing the Fort William Henry siege and surrender (chronicled with greater imagination and fewer facts in James Fenimore Cooper's *Last of the Mohi-*

cans), where he was captured by the Indians. A French officer effected Mason's temporary release, and he was able to escape his captors. He declined a regular commission in the British forces, and after the war removed himself from his home town of Boston to Salem.[33]

By contrast, Timothy Pickering Jr. was Salem born and bred, and came from prosperous if not upper-class stock (his father was a deacon and successful farmer and land speculator). Much of his military career would occur during the Revolution, as Washington's hand-picked commissary general, but in his youth he spent much of his time dodging Salem's dislike for Timothy Pickering Sr.—a man of sharp words and uncompromising moral stances (e.g., he abhorred alcoholic beverages and hated slavery). Righteous, and sometimes rigid, the son had fixed opinions (if not always the same as his father's). Timothy was educated at Harvard College, which he intensely disliked. He graduated in 1763 at age eighteen and returned to Salem. Without his father's wealth but carrying much of his father's blunt and awkward personality, moving up was hard for the young man. He attached himself to the town's grandees and acted the part of a knee-jerk loyalist, but after the Stamp Act riots he began to have second thoughts. He found a new patron in Richard Derby Sr. and edged toward the popular party.[34]

Pickering's attacks on the loyalist faction were sharply worded, but he did not join in the pamphlet wars that had multiplied after 1765. Accused of political opportunism, he defended himself in the language of a gentleman rather than a radical. He simply opposed villainy, self-dealing, and corruption, wherever it appeared, and it now appeared to him in the garment of loyalism. He was a true friend to liberty and proposed to dedicate himself to public service. In that endeavor, he sought public office. When William Browne's militia colonelcy was undone by the mass resignation of his junior officers, Pickering was chosen in his place. In the meantime, Pickering's own personal financial situation deteriorated. But no one could say that he sought office to line his pockets or pass out patronage to his friends. In the end, he was a natural stalwart of the conservative Whig elite: fearful of the mob, determined to maintain control of the town and the colony, and drawn inexorably into the maelstrom of rebellion.[35]

On the other hand, Derby and his sons, mainstays of the emerging patriot faction, stood to gain a great deal by the Whig party's triumph. Though never indicted for it, in all likelihood they had engaged in the time-honored colonial practice of smuggling. British military and financial policy had denied men like the Derbys access to lucrative markets in the French West Indies, and enforcement of the customs acts after 1764 made it harder and more dangerous to smuggle goods from the illicit trade into the colony. While merchants whose primary trade was with British ports had to be persuaded (or coerced) into obeying non-importation, the fishing trade was less affected by non-importation, as its markets were abroad. Derby decided to serve with Pickering when the General Court reassembled in Salem in June of 1774, with the two men ready to pursue more decisive forms of protest.[36]

The General Court met in the town house, "a wooden building, two stories high, of no architectural pretensions, the chambers being occupied by the courts of justice, and the whole area of the lower story, which was supported by columns, was used as a town hall." Led by the Boston delegates, including Samuel Adams and John Hancock, the members were soon debating how to assist beleaguered Boston and protest the parliamentary acts. Adams urged the assembly to call for a continental congress. He had at hand the resolutions of the Boston Committee of Correspondence and the design of the Loyal Nine, a secret group of agitators and insurgents which he led. After some maneuvering, Adams was able to gain a strongly favorable vote for his plan. When Gage learned of this, he sent his secretary, Thomas Flucker, to end the session, but the delegates (Adams leading the way) simply locked the door. Flucker had to read Gage's message aloud in the empty hallway. Samuel Adams, John Adams, James Bowdoin, and Thomas Cushing were selected to attend the first Continental Congress when it assembled in Philadelphia. Bowdoin declined, and Robert Treat Paine was named in his place.[37]

Gage simply did not realize how far the protest had gone and how deeply seated it was. Indeed, he did not really know where Salem's elite stood. Pickering was not designated a delegate, and when the General Court, in defiance of Gage's wishes, voted to comply with the Solemn League and Covenant to boycott British imports, Gage thought that Pickering could act the part of an informant. On June 28th he summoned Pickering and quizzed him. Pickering (according to his own account) did not satisfy the governor, and he was dismissed. Gage found that he could fire off proclamations, and he did. "In observance therefore of my duty to the king," he "enjoin[ed] and command[ed]" the magistrates of the towns to arrest anyone "in any manner entering into or being concerned in such unlawful, hostile, and traitorous combinations," such as Committees of Correspondence, self-styled provincial congresses, and even the Continental Congress, but Gage knew—or should have known—that the magistrates of the towns were the very men they were supposed to arrest.[38]

Gage lingered in the vicinity through the early summer, kept company after July 21st by a detachment of the 64th Regiment of Foot, Colonel Alexander Leslie commanding. They had come from Boston, landed at Marblehead, and marched from Marblehead Harbor up the Country Road, over the Mill Dam bridge at the South River, to camp on swampy Salem Green. The Salem General Court experiment had been a dismal failure from Gage's standpoint, but little did the members of the General Court who barricaded the chamber door against Gage's secretary realize that this was one of the few and the final times that they would have the protest all to themselves. The streets, rather than the chambers of government, were becoming the central scene of the movement. Gage could not even stop the protestors from putting up handbills in the streets of Salem.[39]

But Salem was still home to many loyalists, as the seating at the North (Congregational) Church in Salem, Thomas Barnard Jr.'s congregation, attested. The church stood on the corner of Lynde and North Streets, an imposing two-story building constructed in 1770, with wide aisles within and a rectangular steeple above the gabled entryway. Among his congregation, consisting of fifty-two full members, were numbered the eminent of both parties—patriot stalwarts like ship captain John Felt and Colonel Mason, and loyalists such as Samuel Curwen, William Browne, and numerous members of the Pickman and Nutting clans—and, almost at the back of the church, the merchant Andrew Dalgleish. Though the meetinghouse was without ornament—its purpose was to enable the congregants to hear the sermon, not to enjoy their stay—seating in these meetinghouses was rank ordered. The best men sat closest to the pulpit, and thus to the exposition of the word of God. Children and servants sat in the back or in the gallery. The pulpit was raised so that the entire congregation could hear the minister's sermon, the focal point of worship services. Barnard was but twenty-seven years old, and only two years behind the pulpit, but his father had been pastor before him, and the younger Barnard knew that he must chart a moderate course to please both Whigs and Tories in his congregation.[40]

While the loyalists kept their own counsel, Barnard no doubt urging obedience to God and government on all the members of the church, Gage decided not to convene another session of the runaway General Court. What seemed to him to be the "many tumults and disorders" in the Salem town house—actually not much in the way of tumult as much as a quiet resolve to resist the parliamentary Intolerable Acts—convinced Gage to "excuse and discharge" the elected members. Gage chose his words with excruciating care, hoping to prevent further mischief: "But Salem's representatives were now empowered, with other members of the House, to resolve themselves into a Provincial Congress, which was recommended by the Ipswich Convention." They simply ignored the legally required warrants and oaths (that Gage withheld), named John Hancock of Boston as their speaker, and "passed resolutions" declaring that the governor had violated the colony's constitution "against the express words, as well as the true sense and meaning, of the charter." They assumed that the charter of 1692 was not only still in force, but that it had the status of a constitution, rather than a grant of privileges. "They then resolved themselves into a Congress, and adjourned to meet at Concord on the 11th of October following."[41]

Realizing that Salem's welcome was a chimera, Gage returned to Boston on the 27th of August, followed two weeks later by the two regiments of foot—the 59th and the 64th—that had been quartered in Salem during his sojourn there. The 59th he stationed at Boston Neck, where it might, if necessity dictated, close off the town from the rest of the colony. The 64th returned to Castle Island. At Boston Neck, soldiers constructed fortifications and posted sentries. The incivilities of his stay in Salem put an effective end to civilian negotiations. Gage would continue to address the colony as if he had civil authority, but his only real authority lay in the men under his command. He told the few loyalists who repaired from Salem to Boston that "the unusual warlike preparations throughout the country, make it an act of duty in me to pursue the measures I have taken in constructing what you call a fortress" in Boston. Though he insisted that the capital was open to anyone who wished to enter or leave, it bristled with battlements, cannons, and troops.[42]

While Gage fended off rumors that he intended to bombard the city, the four Massachusetts representatives to the first Continental Congress journeyed to Philadelphia. There they asked for and gained the support of representatives from the other colonies and crafted a petition to the crown for the relief of Boston. The relatively mild measures, in part calculated to retain the support of undecided political leaders, did not appease Gage. He reported to his superiors in England that he had declared the members of the Massachusetts provincial government outlaws. It made no difference to the Whigs, as Gage's reach went only as far as his troops' grasp. William Legge, the second Earl of Dartmouth, was the secretary of state for the Southern Department, including British North America. Lord Dartmouth was not appeased, and he was already thinking about replacing the apparently slow-footed Gage with someone more aggressive. Little did Dartmouth know that his superior, Frederick, Lord North, the prime minister, was losing patience as well. Dartmouth would soon be replaced with the more hawkish Lord Halifax, notwithstanding the fact that North and Dartmouth were stepbrothers (family ties being very prominent among the well-born servants of the crown).[43]

The Massachusetts provincial congress was engaging in the by now time-honored tradition of debating, framing, and petitioning the crown, and across the ocean the king's ministers were preparing to play another round of musical office chairs, while Gage was racking his brains to find a legal solution to the illegality of provincial congresses and continental congresses. Lord Dartmouth offered advice. He wrote to Gage on January 27, 1775, stating that "the essential step to be taken toward reestablishing government would be to arrest and imprison the principal actors and abettors" in these extralegal gatherings. Dartmouth wanted Gage to act the part of a continental policeman, a role that a general with a small force of regular troops could hardly perform.[44]

Gage was caught in a trap not of his own design. He was a military man whose experience ran to giving orders and seeing that they were obeyed, but he was surrounded by an increasingly radicalized citizenry who were leaning toward a far more autonomous way of thinking. He was asked to police a continent, but he had only three thousand soldiers at his command. He could issue proclamations, but he could not enforce them. He could call the General Court into session, but he could not control its deliberations. He watched, more or less helplessly, as Massachusetts's colonial government devolved into a halfway house of self-government. The military solution—the use of force—became his only option. This, and his belief that the colonists would back off from a confrontation with the Regulars, would soon be put to the test.

two Spies Like Us

BRITISH REGULARS were hardly newcomers in the American colonies. Though they were not much trusted, according to prevailing Whig political thinking (standing armies being reviled as the tools of tyrants), the Regulars were key to the British empire's expansion and maintenance. In the eighteenth century, its boundaries were redefined by three great imperial wars, in America styled Queen Anne's War (1703–1713), King George's War (1743–1748), and the French and Indian War (1754–1763)—the latter called the Seven Years' War in Europe. Few troops were deployed before 1755, but after the arrival of General Edward Braddock in Virginia, regiments of Regulars were a nearly continuous and highly visible sign of imperial purpose in America. During the French and Indian War, they came by the tens of thousands, died by the thousands from combat and disease, and defeated French and Indian forces in Pennsylvania, New York, Maine, and, most impressively, in Canada and the West Indies. The Regulars also mingled with civilian populations. For example, awaiting their turn in the 1758–1759 campaign against the French in Canada and the West Indies, British troops were quartered in American port cities like Boston and Charles Town.[1]

Although the colonists' security was based in large measure on the British military commitment to defend the colonies, it was imperial politics and economic competition, rather than military necessity, that led to the last great war for empire in North America. The treaty that ended King George's War in 1748 laid the seeds for the French and Indian War. The pact confirmed the French presence in the upper Northwest and the English claims east of the Appalachian Mountains, but neither power gained control of the Ohio River valley. Hoping to bring to their side all the Indians in that region, the French decided to extend southward the chain of forts they had built along the Great Lakes. The British saw the French initiative as an attempt to stymie British westward expansion. The stage was set for another colonial war.[2]

The colonists then added their own ingredients to the deadly potion. Led by unscrupulous land speculators, the governments of Pennsylvania and Virginia first betrayed and then displaced the Indians in the western portions of their colonies. The colonial governments subsequently gave vast tracts of Indian lands to companies like the Ohio Company of Virginia. Parties of surveyors and hunters, and families of colonists, spread through the Ohio Valley in violation of promises the British authorities made to the Indians. Indians then retaliated with bloody raids and offers of assistance to the French.[3]

After a series of setbacks in the field, a new British government, led by William Pitt, made this war into a European-style conflict, dispatched many regiments of regular troops to America, committed Britain to spend whatever it took to pay for total victory over France in the New World, and pressured the colonies (largely with success) to contribute their share of men, material, and money to the cause. In the summer of 1758, the British took Fort Duquesne (at the forks of the Ohio River), the scene of an earlier British defeat. The French fled. The British struck directly at Canada as well. The door was the St. Lawrence River, and its hinge was still the French fortress of Louisbourg, on Cape Breton Island in Nova Scotia. The British assembled a fleet of thirty-eight warships and an army of twelve thousand soldiers for the assault. The French surrendered on July 17, 1758, after a month of bombardment.

General James Wolfe then led the British troops on an assault of Québec City. Québec's position on the bluffs above the north side of the St. Lawrence menaced traffic on the river. The French garrison, under Montcalm, outnumbered Wolfe's men 15,000 to 12,000, but Wolfe had some of the finest battalions of infantry in British uniform. On September 12th, he led his troops up a narrow natural stairway to the top of the cliffs on which the city sat. Montcalm sallied out with his regulars instead of waiting out a siege, but Wolfe's troops defeated them. Both generals died during the battle. Four days later, the French surrendered the city to the British. The following year a three-pronged attack, with two sets of forces, one from the south and one coming down the St. Lawrence, trapped the French in Montréal. The French capitulated that city on September 7, 1760, nearly a year after Montcalm's men had fled from Wolfe's troops.[4]

Colonial levies had relatively little to do with these victories, reinforcing the British belief that the colonists were not, by nature, soldierly and thus could not win a conflict against a European-led force. The colonists, however, viewed the matter differently. They grew to hate the "lobsterbacks." Even when the tide of war began to change in favor of the British in late 1757, cooperation between British and colonial forces did not breed mutual respect. British officers and soldiers expressed their opinion that the colonial militia and the Indians were untrustworthy and cowardly. As Lieutenant General James Wolfe wrote about the New England militias before the Canadian campaign of 1759: "There is no depending on them in action. . . . Such rascals . . . are rather an encumbrance than any real strength to an army."[5]

Colonial militiamen's sneers notwithstanding, in the French and Indian War the British Regular had proved himself to be a formidable antagonist. By the end of the war, the British Army was the finest land force in North America, a highly experienced, motivated, and well-trained example of a European body operating in a colonial setting. If, earlier in the century, rankers (those of other ranks, i.e., privates and corporals) were poorly treated and officers were poorly trained, the later years of the eighteenth century saw significant reform. Conversely, British officers' dismissive views of the colonial militia notwithstanding, service in the French and Indian War had taught officers like Gage the fearsome tactical effect of individual initiative, smaller formations using the terrain for cover, speedy flanking maneuvers, and other skills that the militia brought to North American warfare. Even if he did not relate the information to his superiors in England, Gage knew that while the British fighting man would give a good account of himself in battle against colonial levies, the task would not be an easy one. As Hugh Percy, commanding the British retreat from Concord on April 19, 1775, later remarked of the colonial militias: "During the whole affair, the rebels attacked us in a very scattered, irregular manner, but with perseverance and resolution, nor did they ever dare to form into a regular body. Indeed they knew too well what was proper, to do so. Whoever looks upon them as an irregular mob, will find himself very much mistaken. They have men amongst them who know very well what they are about, having been employed as rangers against the Indians and Canadians, and this country being very much covered with wood, and hilly, is very advantageous for their method of fighting."[6]

It was thus inevitable but unfortunate that the simmering animosity between colonial and Regular troops, particularly in the officer corps, would lead to errors in British colonial administration in the period prior to the final breach. Mistrust would engender misunderstandings and misperceptions on both sides. Returning militia veterans did not understand the sacrifices that Britons made to keep their troops in the field. By 1760, England had been supporting its European allies against the French in Europe for four years. The British were also attacking French colonies in India, West Africa, and the West Indies. In January 1762, Spain entered the war on France's side. The British then struck at Spanish colonies in Cuba and the Philippines. The burden was enormous, and it could not be borne indefinitely. George II, a supporter of the war effort, died in 1760, and the young King George III favored peace. Diplomats from the warring nations gathered in Paris for peace negotiations. The British kept Canada and the trans-Appalachian west. The French Canadians were allowed to worship as they chose and to keep their titles to their lands. News of the peace brought celebration throughout the British colonies, but Britain still faced a myriad of problems arising from its military commitments. For these had actually expanded as a result of the victory.[7]

To sort these out, George III turned to a career administrator and lawyer, George Grenville. Pompous, long-winded, but incorruptible, his brittle personality and disdainful manner cost him popularity, but his competence with money matters made him valuable at a time when English public finances (that is, the war debt) were in dire straits: hence the Sugar Act of 1764, imposing stricter customs regulations and mechanisms for enforcement, and the hated Stamp Act of 1765. From this point on, the differences in the colonial and the British imperial points of view about the need to pay for military adventures in America became so strident that the British began to think of the need to post troops not on the colonial borders to safeguard the colonists, but in the colonial towns to impose British rule on the colonists.[8]

Adding to the military burden of empire, the Indians, many of whom had been France's allies, distrusted the British and hated the colonists who trespassed on Indian hunting grounds. On May 9, 1763, a force of Indians began a campaign of besieging British forts and burning settlers' homes all along the borderland. But the British garrisons in Detroit, Fort Pitt, and Fort Niagara withstood the assault. "Like a burning brand carried through tinder, the war belts that runners carried from Detroit sparked other attacks in their wake." When the British rushed reinforcements of regular troops and colonial levies to these forts, the Indian marauders backed away. By the winter of 1763/1764, large-scale warfare abated, though peace did not come for two more years. In the Treaty of Fort Stanwix, in 1768, the Indians were forced to give the settlers even more land.[9]

Postwar imperial governance of the North American colonies—based on parliamentary acts and royal placemen like the Indian Affairs supervisors, the customs collectors, and the royal governors—increasingly relied on the British Army and the Royal Navy. The wartime animosity between colonial and British officers poisoned both British and provincial political thinking. Each time the British turned to a military solution, the colonists saw plots and conspiracies against colonial liberties. Each time the colonists protested, the British became more inflexibly committed to military impositions. For example, the Indian rebellion required the infusion of even more British Regulars into the Great Lakes and Ohio Valley regions before it was suppressed. To the planners in Whitehall, the lesson seemed to be that when politics failed, the army would succeed.

The passage of the Quartering Act and the colonial response to the act was an almost perfect example of how combustible this combination of colonial anti-Regular sentiment and British imperial reliance on military governance was. The first Quartering Act, in 1765, was passed (at Gage's suggestion) by Parliament. As commander of the British forces in the colonies, he was perpetually vexed about the problem of finding quarters for his troops. The act provided that troops who could not be housed in barracks could be quartered in private dwellings, "inns, livery stables, ale houses, victualing houses, and the houses of sellers of wine and houses of persons selling of rum, brandy, strong water," as well as in "uninhabited houses, outhouses, barns, or other buildings," with the cost to be borne by colonial legislatures. In 1766, when troops arrived in New York City and Gage sought to house them according to the act, the colony's assembly refused to pay for the lodging, and the troops had to remain on ships in the harbor. A second Quartering Act, in 1774, was designated for the troops going to Boston with Gage and was met with similar hostility.[10]

Thus when disorder erupted in the streets of Boston over the Stamp Act, and later the Townshend Duties, sending troops to the city to quell the unrest was the accepted solution in British imperial thinking, and entirely unacceptable in colonial Whig thinking. In 1768, when the British government sent regular troops to Boston, radicals like Samuel Adams were able to gain a degree of popular support, far exceeding that of the Stamp Act riots, for their opposition activities, because of the deep-seated dislike of British troops. Adams pulled out all the stops to tap into this dislike. He claimed that the troops did not even respect the Sabbath. "The minds of serious people," Adams wrote in an anonymous contribution to the *Journal of the Times*, "this being the Lord's Day, were greatly disturbed with drums beating and fifes playing, unheard of before in this land."[11]

By committing itself to military solutions to political problems, the imperial government had accomplished what the radicals had long desired: it provided an enemy to American liberties so visible in its red coats that no one could miss it. Events threw Gage back to contemplating military solutions to a problem that was inherently political, at the same time as the protesting colonists had convinced many of their countrymen that the very presence of the soldiers was an offense to liberty.

All of this left Gage with little choice in the fall and winter of 1774/1775. His superiors' thinking, channeled and reinforced by the wartime experience of a great victory over the French, was now locked on the military option. He also must have realized that the time his superiors had allotted him to put down the rebellion was growing short. But he had come to know something his masters had not yet fully grasped: the appearance of troops in uniform in the countryside was bound to end badly. He knew he must husband the little discretion he had left. With the mounting provocations of the radicals in the countryside, about which he could do little, he had to deny access to armaments to the colonists.[12]

While Gage was confident that his Regulars would overawe the colonists in face-to-face confrontations, it was best to take no chances with colonial militiamen fighting in Indian fashion by engaging in hit-and run-ambushes from cover. Disarming the colonists entirely was impossible, but limiting their access to artillery and ordnance was within the realm of possibility. Hence the tactic of the gunpowder raid. It was simple, in theory. Until the summer of 1774, Massachusetts towns stored their powder in the Charleston powderhouse, six miles north of Boston. Fearing the confiscation of the colonial gunpowder supply, the towns now began withdrawing their powder. Gage moved swiftly. The operation, on September 1, 1774, went off smoothly, the sheriff turning the keys to the powderhouse over to the 260 men of the 4th Regiment of Foot. The minutemen were hours late. Rumors flew about the colony that more raids were forthcoming. Some of these, like the bombardment of Boston, were pure fiction. Others, like a powder raid at Cambridge, were true, but they did little to reduce the patriots' stock of ammunition. Still, realizing what was happening, the Cambridge militia belatedly assembled and retaliated by destroying the houses of known loyalists in the town, who fled to Boston for safety. With the countryside buzzing like an angry swarm of bees, Gage halted plans for further raids until winter made travel along the roads difficult for the colonial militiamen. Then Gage resumed the raids on Massachusetts and Maine coastal towns. The militia was enraged, but it had arrived too late to deny Gage his gunpowder. At the same time, the colonists were busy with their own gunpowder raids, making off with cannon, shot, and gunpowder stores from a battery on Charles Town Neck on September 8th–9th, and later from Boston itself.[13]

For both sides, the success of gunpowder raids depended on accurate operational intelligence. Gage needed to know what was going on in the countryside, in order to beat the minutemen to the punch. As he wrote to Lord Dartmouth in February 17, 1775, he had "learned from emissaries I have sent through the country" that the rebels were engaging in military exercises, in effect responding to Gage's own military steps with martial responses. The patriots had as many spies in Boston as Gage had in the countryside. With both sides spying on one another, and the loyalties of spies never entirely certain, Gage could only rely on his officers, traveling incognito, for trustworthy information.

Gage set these men the task of surveying potential routes of march, fields of battle, and sites for camps, should open hostilities begin. He did not allow them to wear their uniforms, as the simmering animosity toward the Regulars had come to a rolling boil. Typical of these missions was one scheduled for early February 1775. For it, he turned to two young officers in his command: Captain William Brown of the 52nd Regiment of Foot, and Ensign Henry DeBerniere, an engineering officer of the 10th Regiment whose talents included cartography and surveying. With his characteristic care, Gage laid out their task: "Gentlemen, You will go through the Counties of Suffolk and Worcester, taking a sketch of the country as you pass; it is not expected you should make out regular plans and surveys, but mark out the roads and distances from town to town, as also the situation and nature of the country; all passes must be particularly laid down, noticing the length and breadth of them, the entrance in and going out of them, and whether to be avoided by taking other routes." What Gage had in mind was determining how many men could quickly regain the ordnance the colonists had secreted away. How to carry the cannons back to him was a second problem. Road travel with such heavy loads would be slow, and it would expose the soldiers to attack. Perhaps the raiders could use flat-bottomed barges on waterways? "The rivers also to be sketched out, remarking their breadth and depth and the nature of their banks on both sides, the fords, if any, and the nature of their bottoms, many of which particulars may be learned of the country people." Gage was thinking about colonial resistance to his raids when he added a request for information about terrain: "You will remark the heights you meet with, whether the ascents are difficult or easy; as also the woods and the mountains, with the height and nature of the latter, whether to be got round or easily passed over. The nature of the country to be particularly noticed, whether inclosed or open, if the former, what kind of inclosures," all of which could provide cover for minutemen lurking about (just like the Indians). If a full-scale intrusion were necessary, or if the raiders had to be rescued by a larger force, the two officers were to discover "whether the country admits of making roads for troops on the right or left of the main road, or on the sides. You will notice the situation of the towns and villages, their churches and church yards, whether they are advantageous spots to take post in, and capable of being made defensible." Finally, if war came, Gage would need to know one other essential item: "If any places strike you as proper for encampments, or appear strong by nature, you will remark them particularly, and give reasons for your opinions. It would be useful if you could inform yourselves of the necessaries the different counties could supply, such as provisions, forage, straw, &c. the number of cattle, horses etc. in the several townships."[14]

Gage knew that victory in a long war depended on what happened behind the lines of battle. The British Army could control the coastline with the aid of the Royal Navy, but the value of the empire lay in its hinterlands: its farms and plantations. The staple products of these agrarian factories—rice, sugar, tobacco, wheat, corn, livestock, timber, and timber products, in addition to beaver pelts and deerskins—had made the imperial venture profitable. An empire whose authority did not penetrate into the interior was a waste of Britain's time and money. To subdue a rebellion in the countryside thus required the ability to maneuver freely through the interior. But the vast spaces and rugged landscape of North America's interior would make such a war a gamble without reliable information on the terrain and the local population.

Gage thought the two men were suited for the mission because of their personal abilities, but his reasons for this assessment are lost to history. A remarkable account of their adventure as spies in the days leading up to the Salem gunpowder raid nevertheless affords some idea of those talents. A copy, based on DeBerniere's journal, was left in the hands of a printer in 1779 and published as "The Spies' Story of Their Trip to Worcester." Because of the by-now entrenched hatred of former wartime colonial officers—who had become the leaders of their towns—and serving British officers, the reconnaissance took on the color of an espionage mission.[15]

DeBerniere opened the account with Gage's orders. In "the latter end of February, 1775 [actually the 22nd], Captain Brown and myself received orders to go through the counties of Suffolk and Worcester, and sketch the roads as we went, for the information of General Gage, as he expected to have occasion to march troops through that country the ensuing spring." Gage's plan of a second series of gunpowder raids might bring the colonists to their senses. It was as much a way to forestall wider conflict as to give Britain an advantage should a more general war begin. The journal suggests that it was general knowledge among the officers of the garrison that Gage was planning a gunpowder raid to the interior of the colony.

"We set out from Boston on Thursday, disguised like countrymen, in brown clothes and reddish handkerchiefs round our necks; at the ferry of Charlestown, we met a sentry of the 52nd Regiment, but Captain Brown's servant, whom we took along with us, bid him not take any notice of us, so that we passed unknown to Charlestown." The sentries were posted to watch and warn Gage about any militia activity, but they could not stray far from their barracks—it was too dangerous. Brown and DeBerniere also must have realized how dangerous their mission was, but DeBerniere did not report on their feelings.

Instead, the journal reads as a kind of travelogue, with a twist, for everywhere that the two spies went, they saw a people armed and dangerous. One can follow the two men virtually, on a tour through eastern Massachusetts in the last days of empire there.

"We went to Cambridge, a pretty town, with a college built of brick, the ground is entirely level on which the town stands." A colonial college was in essence a single building that housed the students, classrooms, a small library, and a place for students to take their meals. By 1775 Harvard College, already 139 years old, consisted of Harvard Hall (rebuilt after the catastrophic fire of 1764) and Massachusetts Hall (originally built in 1720), classroom buildings; Stoughton Hall and Hollis Hall, dormitories; Holden Chapel; and Wadsworth House, the home of the president of the college. The ministerial, mercantile, and legal elite of the colony had matriculated and graduated from the college, with both loyalists and patriots boasting of Harvard degrees.[16]

On the road, the two officers and Brown's batman (an officer's personal servant) tried to be inconspicuous, fitting in with the many native-born and immigrant young men who had no prospects. Much of eastern Massachusetts's farmland, subdivided and passed from father to son for 150 years, left little for the revolutionary generation to own, and less was available for the flood of immigrants pouring into the colonies after the French and Indian War. The able poor went from town to town looking for work as laborers— hence the British officers' disguise of plain woolen work clothes and bandannas. Ironically, on the evening of April 18th, when Paul Revere's comrade William Dawes rode out of Boston to warn the countryside that the Regulars were coming, he, too, adopted the costume of a Humphrey Ploughjogger, an ordinary country laborer. The British sentries on Boston Neck took no notice of Dawes.[17]

In fact, both sides were engaged in a full-time competition of intelligence gathering. For every spy that Gage sent into the countryside or that came to his headquarters in Boston, the Whigs had ten: volunteers loosely organized around the Committees of Safety in the various towns; militia officers in the counties; fast riders who carried messages from village to village; and, most importantly, Revere's network of mechanics, craftsmen, and professionals (including doctors and ministers) who kept a keen eye on Gage and the troops in Boston. The advantage that the colonists exercised was in numbers, not in the quality of their information. They had no one inside Gage's entourage and had to guess at his plans from the disposition and movement of his men. The colonial networks thus spread rumor as swiftly as information. The advantage that Gage had was the quality of the information he obtained, but it was often out of date by the time it reached him. What was more vexing was the danger that his agents would be recognized for what they were—officers in disguise.

Brown, DeBerniere, and Dawes all hoped that by dressing down in the costume of ordinary workers, they could become almost invisible. It was a perfect inversion of the rituals of wearing a military uniform. The red coats of the Regulars made them highly visible, because the observer was supposed to be cowed. The soldiers' marching in step reinforced the impression of solidity. Uniforms visibly foregrounded the troops. By leaving their uniforms behind, the spies more readily merged with the background.

DeBerniere continued, "We next went to Watertown, and were not suspected." Which is to say, the two officers did not notice whether they were attracting unwanted attention; at least no one was looking hard at them. "It is a pretty large town for America, but would be looked upon as a village in England." In fact, by tax assessments and population, Watertown bowed only to Salem and Boston in its grandeur. The largest cities in the British North American colonies were Boston, New York City, Philadelphia, and Charles Town, with Philadelphia's 40,000 people first and foremost. Boston had 16,000, although the numbers are merely estimates. The average population of a New England town would have been less than 1,000 inhabitants. Everyone would have known just about everyone else, although newcomers were also common, for the colonial population after the French and Indian War was soaring.[18]

"A little out of this town we went into a tavern, a Mr[.] Brewer's, a Whig." The division of colonists into Whigs (the protestors against Parliament) and those who were loyal to the British government was by now almost complete. Some colonial leaders, such as Connecticut lawyer William Samuel Johnson, New York lawyer William Smith Jr., and Philadelphia lawyer Joseph Galloway, tried to find a middle ground that would guarantee American legal rights within the British Empire, but their efforts at compromise to prevent what Smith called this "unnatural contest" had no traction. Men like Galloway would find themselves (so they later told Parliament), "inhumanly treated." At any rate, both sides seemed bent on confrontation.[19]

"We called for dinner, which was brought in by a black woman; at first she was very civil, but afterwards began to eye us very attentively; she then went out and a little after returned, when we observed to her that it was a very fine country, upon which she answered 'So it is, and we have got brave fellows to defend it; and if you go up any higher you will find it so.'" A bold comment for a serving woman, but, in context, a warning. "Go up any higher" meant go any farther into the countryside. "This disconcerted us a good deal, and we imagined she knew us from our papers which we took out before her, as the General had told us to pass for Surveyors; however, we resolved not to sleep there that night, as we had intended; accordingly we paid our bill which amounted to £2 odd shillings, but it was Old Tenor."

The papers were probably rough drafts of maps rather than surveyors' drawings, but the two men did not have surveyors' equipment, making the purpose of the maps suspicious. The Old Tenor bills, issued before 1750 by the General Court, were also suspicious, for only a few were still in circulation. The workmen's disguise had not worked, nor had the ruse that the two men were surveyors. DeBerniere was trained as a military engineer to survey land, but the two men were not carrying a surveyor's compass and map table, much less rods and chains. Still, it seemed worth a try. As land hunger gobbled up much of western Massachusetts, skilled surveyors found a ready market for their services. It was an honorable profession. George Washington, for example, was a much-sought-after surveyor in Virginia. It was this skill that induced the royal governor to offer Washington an officer's commission and send him to the forks of the Ohio River to spy on the French in 1753.[20]

For reasons yet to be revealed, the black servant at the tavern did not like the look of the newcomers, and she reported them. The word "servant" might mean someone in a servile occupation, but more likely it was a euphemism for "slave." In 1765, there were 5,253 adult slaves in Massachusetts, most working alongside free persons in domestic service, at the docks, or as cartmen. They talked openly among themselves about freedom, and when the Declaration of Independence was read throughout Massachusetts, the slaves prepared their own petition for freedom, based on the Declaration's preamble. For the present, the countryside policed itself with a watch-and-warn system, of which the slaves were an unofficial part. Even though a black bondwoman could not join the *posse comitatus*, she would be rewarded for passing on the information.[21]

The officers were worried about her. "After we had left the house we inquired of John, our servant, what she had said; he told us that she knew Captain Brown very well; that she had seen him five years before at Boston, and knew him to be an officer, and that she was sure I was one also." That was sufficient to cause alarm, but John's report was not done. She thought him a Regular, though "he denied it." Finally, "she said she knew our errand was to take a plan of the country; that she had seen the river and road through Charlestown on the paper; she also advised him to tell us not to go any higher, for if we did we should meet with very bad usage." The tavernkeeper's servant would have made an excellent spy herself, and her comments nearly put an abrupt end to the mission. "Upon this we called a Council, and agreed that if we went back we should appear very foolish, as we had a great number of enemies in town [i.e., Boston], because the General had chose to employ us in preference to them; it was absolutely necessary to push on to Worcester, and run all risk, rather than go back until we are forced." Apparently, acting the role of a spy was a road to preferment among the officer corps, and the appointment of Brown and DeBerniere had aroused the envy of their fellow officers. Had the troops more to do with their time than just garrison duty, they might not have engaged in such petty jealousies, but their desire to be out and doing was still unfulfilled. There was even some grumbling directed at what seemed to be Gage's timidity. Thus when Gage selected Brown and DeBerniere, animosity toward him fell on them.

One notes that the account did not include the name of the black serving woman, but it reported the conversation as being between the two servants, perhaps because the officers belonged to a higher social stratum than the servants. Servants might chafe at these distinctions, but they were well understood. Free workers in the colonies, however, were becoming far less concerned with deference to their betters by this time, displaying a surliness and temper that frightened men of substance. Since the officers were unable to fit in with the lower orders (their accents would have given them away, whatever costumes they donned), they had to suspect everyone of betraying their mission. "We continued our route, and went about six miles further; we met a country fellow driving a team, and a fellow with him whom we suspected to be a deserter; they both seemed very desirous to join company with us, and told us, upon our saying we were going towards Worcester, that they were going our way." The officers declined the offer.[22]

Companionship on the road was common—walking, talking, sharing food and drink and stories. One could never tell if one's congenial companion was what he said he was, however. Travelers reported that their sometime companions were entirely untrustworthy. One had to listen carefully before one shared a confidence. As Dr. Alexander Hamilton of Annapolis, Maryland, traveled about the colonies for his health in 1743, he took careful and often caustic note of the speech of his traveling companions. At the outset of his journey, someone named Hart took Hamilton to a house and there they "drank some punch and conversed like a couple of virtuosos." On the road, Mr. Dean, a minister, only offered "rambling conversation." Hamilton's landlord's contribution was "so very lumpish and heavy that it disposed me mightily to sleep." Fortunately for the doctor, not all the innkeepers droned on. In Newtown, Maryland, "a deal of comical discourse passed in which the landlord, a man of particular talent at telling comic stories, bore the chief part." Hamilton's exchange with a New Light zealot named, inappropriately, Thomas Quiet, ended in an argument: "He told me flatly that I was damned without redemption." From their manner of speech Hamilton could tell (or thought he could) his traveling companions' learning, background, and re-finement, though some fooled him. William Morrison, whose speech pro-claimed him a "plain, homely fellow" had "good linen in his bags, [with] a pair of silver buckles, silver clasps, and gold sleeve buttons." Hamilton's as-sumption that speech made the man was shared by the many who could tell "a person of more than ordinary rank" by that individual's "polite conversa-tion." Before a man who proffered the latter, the lower sort "know as well as others how to fawn and cringe." One had to listen carefully, and the spies did not like what they heard.[23]

But they had their orders and pressed on. "As we began to suspect some-thing, we stopt at a tavern at the Sign of the Golden Ball with an intention to get a drink, and so proceed; but upon our going in the landlord pleased us so much, as he was not inquisitive, that we resolved to lye there that night; so we ordered some fire to be made in the room we were in, and a little after to get us some coffee; he told us we might have what we pleased, either tea or coffee." The offer of tea was a code, for the non-importation agreements had targeted the hated leaf of the East India Company. The landlord was hint-ing that he was a loyalist. "We immediately found out with whom we were, and were not a little pleased to find, on some conversation, that he was a friend to Government, a son of the Tory, Col. Elisha Jones. He told us that he had been very ill used by them sometime before; but that since he had shewed them that he was not to be bullied, they had left him pretty quiet." The officers could now seek and rely on information from the tavernkeeper. "We then asked him for the inns that were on the road between his house and Worcester; he recommended us to two, one at about nine miles from his house, a Mr[.] Buckminster's, and another at Worcester, a namesake of his own, a Mr[.] [Isaac] Jones."

Taverns and inns along the roads were places of rough equality in New England. At inns, the high seat backs of booths, helping to keep conversations from prying ears, were an alternative to the traditional long tables, where everyone could hear everyone else. The visitor hoped for decent victuals and a snug rope–box-spring bed (hence the saying "sleep tight"). Silas Deane of Wethersfield, Connecticut, traveling to the first Continental Congress, wrote to his wife Elizabeth about one experience: "The tavern appeared tolerable . . . but to our surprise here was no fruit, bad rum, and nothing of the meat kind but salt pork. . . . I called for bread[,] cheese[,] and porter [a strong ale] . . . but I could not taste them so rotten were they." Even in the friendly confines of Jones's inn, the two spies had to be careful who was listening, for the minutemen regarded taverns as convenient places in which to gather.[24]

New England weather is variable in winter. Fine, sunny days can turn nasty, cold, and wet very quickly, as the travelers discovered. "The second day was very rainy and a kind of frost with it; however we resolved to set off, and accordingly we proceeded to Mr[.] [Joseph] Buckminster's; we met nothing extraordinary on the road; we passed some time in sketching a pass[age?] that lay on the road; and of consequence were very dirty and wet on our arrival. On our entering the house we did not much like the appearance of things; we asked for dinner and they gave us some sausages; we praised everything exceedingly, which pleased the old woman of the house much; they gave us a room to ourselves, which was what we wanted; after being there some time we found we were pretty safe, as by that time we perceived that the *cote de pays* was not a dangerous one; of consequence we felt very happy, and Brown, I, and our man John, made a very happy supper; for we always treated him as our companion, since our adventure with the black woman."

Like the sidekick in the picaresque novels so popular at the time, John the servant had earned his master's trust. So had Sancho Panza—a little roguish, with a quick wit, a ready tongue, and skills his master would never ply— gained the trust of Don Quixote. If one considers the spies' tale a work of literature as well as a report to a superior, some of the themes that might otherwise be buried in it appear in sharper relief. The good-hearted and loyal servant is one of these. John protects his master and the ensign, watching out for their safety, and keeps an ear open behind the stairs, in the alley, and on the road. The connection between the black female servant and the white male servant was another theme in eighteenth-century literature, where illicit love, vengeance, and miscegenation titillated English audiences.[25]

"We slept there that night, and the next morning, being a very fine one, we resolved to push on to Worcester, which was about thirty miles from us; we proceeded about nine miles without anything extraordinary happening, except meeting two men whom we suspected to be deserters. We then dined in the woods on a tongue and some cherry brandy we brought with us, and we changed our stockings, which refreshed us much, our feet being very wet. We then travelled through a very fine country, missed our way and went to Westborough; we were obliged to turn back a mile to get the right road. We then passed through Shrewsbury; all a fine, open, cultivated country. We came into a pass about four miles from Worcester, where we were obliged to stop to sketch."

Military officers' sketches of cities and the countryside provide some of the most detailed and accurate maps of the eighteenth-century colonies. The surveyors' papers provided the excuse for the sketches, but military purposes were foremost in Brown's and Gage's thinking. Skills mastered and practiced in England and Scotland, as well as those deployed in eighteenth-century European warfare, proved that accurate mapping was vital to the success of operations. Engineers in uniform were the most common mapmakers, their cartography designed to determine the best places for encampments and roads, and to reveal obstacles to military maneuvers.[26]

"We arrived at Worcester at five o'clock in the afternoon, very much fatigued." It is nearly fifty miles from Boston to Worcester, and the officers had made good time. "The people in the town did not take notice of us as we came in, so we got safe to Mr[.] Jones's tavern; on our entrance he seemed a little sour, but it wore off by degrees and we found him to be our friend, which made us very happy; we dined [the early-evening meal] and supped [a late-evening meal] without anything happening out of the common run." DeBerniere only reported sporadically on his conversation with Brown. Such a mission might lead to bonding; alternatively, little irritations might become big ones. DeBerniere hints that the two men trusted one another and had become accustomed to one another's companionship.

"The next day being Sunday, we could not think of travelling, as it was contrary to the custom of the country; nor dare we stir out until the evening because of Meeting [i.e., the townspeople going to church], and no body is allowed to walk the streets during divine service without being taken up and examined; so that thinking we could not stand the examination so well, we thought it prudent to stay at home, where we wrote and corrected our sketches." Attendance at church on the Sabbath was required by Massachusetts law, but that law was no longer strictly enforced. The Congregational church was still established in the colony, and taxes went to pay for ministers of that denomination, but the Church of England (Episcopal), the Baptists, the Methodists, the Quakers, and other nonconformists also worshiped in the colony. Roman Catholics, before 1692 forbidden to set foot in Massachusetts, still labored under various burdens (priests were not allowed to celebrate Mass), but there were Catholics in the colony. The proliferation of sects weakened the impact of the attendance regulations. Men and women, particularly the young, could be found in public places outside of churches during the morning and afternoon services, but dancing, playing games, gambling, and drinking were still offenses presented by grand juries, and transgressors were fined accordingly. Thus if one did not attend services, it was best to remain out of sight.[27]

The tea code was once again employed, but Brown and DeBerniere did not want to share too much information with the tavernkeeper. This need-to-know rule was as old as the first spies. "The landlord was very attentive to us, and on our asking what he could give us for breakfast, he told us tea or anything else we chose—that was an open confession [to] what he was; but for fear he might be imprudent, we did not tell him who we were, though we were certain he knew it." Tavernkeepers readily joined in the political conversations of their patrons, read the newspapers aloud and commented on them, and were not above spreading rumor and gossip from one patron to another.[28]

The two officers waited until the churchgoers had returned home from the afternoon services. "In the evening we went round the town and on all the hills that command it, sketched everything we desired, and returned to the town without being seen. That evening about eight o'clock the landlord came in and told us that there were two gentlemen who wanted to speak with us; we asked him who they were; on which he said we would be safe in their company; we said we did not doubt that, as we hoped that two gentlemen who travelled merely to see the country and stretch our limbs, as we had lately come from sea, could not meet with anything else but civility, when we behaved ourselves properly." It was late, and in winter the deep darkness had already come, but visiting taverns was a tradition among New England males, and there was nothing untoward in the invitation. Indeed, the tavernkeeper might have incautiously told fellow loyalists about the officers and wanted them to share what they knew (or, more likely, a litany of their complaints) with Brown and DeBerniere. "He told us he would come in again in a little time and perhaps we would change our minds, and then left us."

In fact, that was the case. "An hour [later] he returned, and told us the Gentlemen were gone, but had begged him to let us know, as they knew us to be officers of the army, that all their friends of Government at Petersham were disarmed by the rebels, and that they threatened to do the same at Worcester in a very little time; he sat and talked politics, and drank a bottle of wine with us, and also told us that none but a few friends to Government knew we were in town; we said it was very indifferent to us whether they did or not, though we thought very differently; however, as we imagined we had staid long enough in that town we resolved to set off at day break the next morning and get to Framingham." Worcester was a stronghold of the Whig faction by this time, the loyalists there having been driven out or to cover. Gage's chosen councillors, the judges of the superior court, and everyone else who openly accepted the authority of the crown were thoroughly cowed by violence or the threat of violence.[29]

Wisely, the three Englishmen were on foot. Had they been on horseback, their identity would have been immediately suspected. English officers rode; rankers walked. But the disguises had worn thin: perhaps because all strangers were suspect, perhaps because the officers' accents were a little different from the townspeople this far west, perhaps because deserters from the regiments in Boston had informed on the spies.

The last of these surmises was soon confirmed. "Off we set, after getting some roast beef and brandy from our landlord, which was very necessary on a long march, and prevented us going into houses where perhaps they might be too inquisitive." Breakfast in New England was usually porridge and milk or, if one was lucky with one's host, cold meat. Bread and butter might be added to the menu, along with cheese, fruits in season (often baked in pies), and, more rarely, eggs and salted pork products. The addition of the brandy was a treat, but American meals were often accompanied by cider, beer, wine (for the upper classes), and other alcoholic beverages. It was far safer to drink these than the water.[30]

Thus refreshed, "we took a road we had not come, and that led us to the pass four miles from Worcester." Unlike the improved roads along the coast, sometimes called king's highways, and the high streets in towns, roads in the New England interior hardly deserved that name. These roads, which connected village to town and town to town, followed cow paths and old Indian trails; were rarely straight for longer than a quarter mile, twisting through a patchwork of fields, marshes, wooded copses, and hillside; were rutted; and were dusty in summer, muddy in spring and fall, and snow-covered in winter. Even on the edge of the town, the roads were rarely wider than the width of a cart, despite the fact that the use of wheeled farm vehicles was the reason why roads were necessary. Owners of lots adjacent to the road were required to tend to the road's upkeep and were fined by local courts when, as was often the case, they allowed brush and other impediments to traffic to collect on the road. Local knowledge, rather than maps, directed travelers over these roads, as the two officers were discovering. One did not travel the roads, one "defied" them.[31]

Using back roads, "we went on unobserved by any one until we had passed Shrewsbury, where we were overtaken by a horseman [later identified as Captain Timothy Bigelow, a Worcester militia commander] who examined us very attentively, and especially me, whom he looked at from head to foot as if he wanted to know me again; after he had taken his observations he rode off pretty hard and took the Marlborough road, but by good luck we took the Framingham road again to be more perfect in it, as we thought it would be the one made use of."

Massachusetts law allowed magistrates to closely examine men and women entering a town. The warning-out system was old, borrowed from English parish-officers' duties and carried to Massachusetts in the seventeenth century. Towns were responsible for the destitute, and seemingly sturdy beggars were discouraged from venturing farther into the town. Young men were especially suspect, and, as the spies had elected to appear of the "middling sort," their work prospects were the subject of official concern. Thus Bigelow was simply reenacting the office that selectmen routinely performed. Yet Bigelow's rideabout in search of deserters, spies, and criminals on the roads worried the spies, and the tenor of his examination convinced them to be even more circumspect in their contact with the locals. As it happened, on March 14, 1775, the Massachusetts Provincial Congress instructed Bigelow to add inspection of the armories in the country to his other militia duties.[32]

For Bigelow held another office. He was a member of the Committee of Safety. The first Committee of Safety was chosen on October 27, 1774, with three members from Boston and six others from the surrounding counties. Its task was to watch and warn, and it could call out the militia when necessary.

At first it did not have formal police powers, but a reorganization on February 9, 1775, enlarged the committee to eleven and gave committee members and any posse they assembled the duty "to observe and inspect any and all persons" who might try to effectuate the Intolerable Acts. The committee knew by now that the two men were officers of the British Army. Had they been civilians, they might well have faced the "rough music" that locals had imposed on their loyalist neighbors. No shots had been exchanged between Gage's forces and the militia. After Lexington and Concord, "British soldiers who fell into American hands were treated as enemies," but in late February to have captured and ill treated two officers of the British Army would have been an act of war, which might have brought serious consequences. Better, then, to harry and frighten the officers without touching them, and that is exactly what the horsemen, the outriders, the villagers, and the patriot leaders did.[33]

A close encounter of a similar kind awaited the spies in Framingham. "We arrived at Buckminster's tavern about six o'clock that evening. The company of Militia were exercising near the house, and an hour after they came and performed their feats before the windows of the room we were in; we did not feel very easy at seeing such a number so very near us; however, they did not know who we were, and took little or no notice of us." British officers' low opinion of colonial militia had, if anything, grown after the French and Indian War. For the Regulars, the parade, with the trooping of the colors, was a version of the column marching toward battle. For the militia, it was a social occasion as much as a martial one. Brown and DeBerniere concluded that the militia ran on oratory and alcohol. "After they had done their exercise, one of their commanders spoke a very eloquent speech, recommending patience, coolness and bravery (which indeed they much wanted); particularly told them they would always conquer if they did not break; and recommended them to charge us coolly, and wait for our fire, and everything would succeed with them. . . . After so learned and spirited [a] harangue, he dismissed the parade, and the whole company came into the house and drank until nine o'clock, and then returned to their respective homes full of pot-valor."

Whatever the quality of the militia during the French and Indian War, the institution of the militia muster was a central part of social experience in the towns. Drinking at the tavern might seem a poor preparation for battle, but it brought the men together and bonded them. Although one historian argued that the militia in New England was poorly armed and could not use their muskets, most scholars believe the contrary. In the winter of 1775, after Leslie's retreat, Timothy Pickering compiled a return of the Salem militia's firearms. Of the 618 men who mustered for the militia, every one reported with a firearm. While the 100 percent figure was unusual, other Massachusetts militia formations returned over 90 percent. Moreover, the colonial officers were willing learners of the military arts. In a manual he compiled for militia exercises, Pickering conceded something very much like the British spies' opinions of the militia's abilities. "I have been somewhat used to firearms—have had a little experience in the militia—and am in some degree acquainted with the difficulties in training up the men in military knowledge, in the short time which either the laws or their own inclinations shall induct them to attend military exercises." But he was willing to hold the office, and knew his men would fight, if it came to that.[34]

The spies kept their opinion of the militia to themselves. "We slept there that night and nobody in the house suspected us. Next morning we set off for Weston, had a very agreeable day, having fine weather and a beautiful country to travel through; we met nothing extraordinary on the road; nobody knew us, and we were asked very few questions. On our arrival at Mr[.] Jones's we met with a very welcome reception, he being our friend; we received several hints from the family not to attempt to go on any more into the country; but as we had succeeded so well heretofore, we were resolved to go the Sudbury road [the main road that led to Worcester], and go as far as the thirty seven Milestone, where we had left the main road and taken the Framingham road. We slept at Jones's that night, and got all our sketches together and sent them to Boston with our man, so that if they did stop and search us, they would not get our papers."

The spies' account suggests that all of the operational intelligence they had gathered was entrusted to Brown's man John, and he carried it to Gage in Boston. While that is possible, entrusting a servant with such an important and dangerous task, without supervision, so far from the British enclave, over roads and through countryside that the servant had only just reconnoitered, seems improbable. This detail, like some others in the account, does stretch the reader's credulity, but unlikely choices of messengers and couriers abound in the history of spying. In any case, John no longer appeared in the journal.

More bad weather slowed the spies, but it would prove to be their salvation. "The next day was very cloudy and threatened bad weather, towards twelve o'clock it snowed; we dined soon in hopes the weather would clear up,—at two o'clock it ceased snowing a little, and we resolved to set off for Marlborough, which was about sixteen miles off; we found the roads very bad, every step up to our ankles." Poor colonial roads were hardly a novelty to the spies by this time; they could have predicted terrible road conditions. But southern New England weather could never be predicted. Snowfalls might accumulate to over the height of a man, and though the winter of 1774/1775 was not notable for its blizzards, the variability of weather presented its own hazards. People froze to death in sudden storms, or lost their way and died from starvation. One ventured forth at one's own risk in winter.[35]

The spies were lucky to be able to keep to the road. "We passed through Sudbury, a very large village, near a mile long, the causeway lies across a great swamp, or overflowing of the river Sudbury, and commanded by a high ground on the opposite side." Another hazard of traveling these roads was sudden flooding. The New Englanders practiced clear-cutting of woodlands and deep plowing of fields, which increased the risk of flooding. "Nobody took the least notice of us until we arrived within three miles of Marlborough (it was snowing hard all the while), when a horseman overtook us and asked us from whence we came, we said from Weston, he asked if we lived there, we said no; he then asked us where we resided, and as we found there was no evading his questions, we told him we lived at Boston." Strangers were always suspect: then, as spies; today, as criminals. The entire countryside seemed to have been alerted to the officers' presence. "He then asked us where we were going, we told him to Marlborough, to see a friend (as we intended to go to Mr[.] Barnes's, a gentleman to whom we were recommended, and a friend to Government)." The horseman, like Bigelow, was looking for the two men. "He then asked us if we were in the army, we said not, but were a good deal alarmed at his asking us that question; he asked several rather impertinent questions, and then rode on for Marlborough, as we suppose, to give them intelligence there of our coming." In Marlborough, Brown and DeBerniere found the townspeople turned out, and not in welcome. "For on our entering the town, the people came out of their houses (though it snowed and blew very hard) to look at us, in particular a baker asked Captain Brown, 'Where are you going, Master?' [and] he answered 'On to see Mr[.] Barnes.'"

The baker knew that Brown was not what he seemed (hence he called him Master). Indeed, the entire town knew about the identities of the two men, but their purpose was still not discovered. They might be deserters seeking a safe place to stay. The two officers, in turn, knew that their time in country was growing short. Barnes was more than a contact; he was, hope-fully, a sanctuary. According to contemporary sources, Henry Barnes, "a wealthy distiller and importer," lived in a substantial dwelling at the edge of Marlborough. He had connections to Britain that could not be thrown off easily ("his sister Elizabeth had married Nathaniel Coffin, the last receiver-general and cashier of his Majesty's customs"). Barnes employed village peo-ple and, in quieter times, would have been a selectman himself. He was later banished for his correctly suspected sympathies.[36]

"We proceeded to Mr[.] Barnes's, and on our beginning to make an apol-ogy for taking the liberty to make use of his house and discovering to him that we were officers in disguise, he told us we need not be at the pains of telling him, that he knew our situation, that we were very well known (he was afraid) by the town's people.—We begged he would recommend some tavern where we should be safe, he told us we could be safe no where but in his house; that the town was very violent, and that we had been expected at Colo. Williams's the night before, where there had gone a party of liberty people to meet us."

Violence against loyalists was sporadic. For example, loyalist Israel Wil-liams of Hatfield, Massachusetts, some eighty miles as the crow flies to the west of Marlborough, was watched but not yet harmed. He had distinguished himself as a militia officer in the colonial wars, and he represented the town as a selectman and the county as a judge, as well as sitting in the governor's council. In general, if a person if substance was a loyalist, he might stave off retaliation if he was well liked, or take oaths to the new government and es-cape persecution. When the going became too hot, even the most prudent of loyalists took flight to Boston. Williams was sought and arrested in 1777, but he remained in the colony, and his descendants would help fund the creation of Williams College.[37]

"We suspected, and indeed had every reason to believe, that the horse-man that met us and took such particular notice of me, the morning we left Worcester, was the man who told them we should be at Marlborough the night before, but our taking the Framingham road when he had passed us, deceived him—Whilst we were talking, the people were gathering in little groups in every part of the town.—Mr[.] Barnes asked us who had spoke to us on our coming into the town, we told him a baker; he seemed a little star-tled at that, told us he was a mischievous fellow, and that there was a deserter at his house; Captain Brown asked the man's name, he said it was Swain, that he had been a drummer; Brown knew him too well, as he was a man of his own company, and had not been gone above a month."

Desertion from Gage's regiments had grown to serious proportions. Rations in Boston were in short supply, pay was irregular, and the temptation to depart almost too easy (lose the uniform and cross the neck of land connecting Boston to the mainland in a crowd of workers, perhaps). Gage had already issued one proclamation offering pardon to returnees and serious punishment to those who stayed out. Some availed themselves of the pardon and then disappeared. These two officers did not desert, but they were bewildered by Gage's apparent leniency with the colonists.[38]

"So we found we were discovered.—We asked Mr[.] Barnes if they did get us into their hands, what they would do with us; he did not seem to like to answer; we asked him again, he then said we knew the people very well, that we might expect the worst of treatment from them.—Immediately after this, Mr[.] Barnes was called out; he returned a little after and told us the doctor of the town [possibly Dr. Samuel Curtis, of the Committee of Correspondence] had come to tell him he was come to sup with him—(now this fellow had not been within Mr[.] Barnes's doors for two years before, and came now for no other business than to see and betray us)—Barnes told him he had company and could not have the pleasure of attending him that night; upon this the fellow stared about the house and asked one of Mr[.] Barnes's children who her father had got with him, the child innocently answered that she had asked her Pappa, but he told her it was not her business; he then went, I suppose to tell the rest of his crew."

It was time to return to Boston. The problem was how to get there undetected. "When we found we were in that situation, we resolved to lie down for two or three hours, and set off at twelve o'clock at night; so we got some supper on the table and were just beginning to eat, when Barnes (who had been making enquiry of his servants) found they intended to attack us, and then he told us plainly he was very uneasy for us, that we could be no longer in safety in that town." Barnes, like the officers, knew that there were two sources of information: upstairs, among people of means, and downstairs, among the servants. Without John, the spies had no access to the latter. "We resolved to set off immediately, and asked Mr[.] Barnes if there was no road round the town, so that we might not be seen; he took us out of his house by the stables, and directed us to a bye road which was to lead us a quarter of a mile from the town." Now the weather closed in, and a New England snowstorm can very quickly become a whiteout. "It snowed and blew as much as ever I see it in my life; however, we walked pretty fast, fearing we should be pursued; at first we felt much fatigued, having not been more than twenty minutes at Mr[.] Barnes's to refresh ourselves, and the roads (if possible) were worse than when we came; but in a little time after it wore off, and we got [away] without being perceived, as far as the hills that command the causeway at Sudbury, and went into a little wood where we eat a bit of bread that we took from Mr[.] Barnes's, and eat a little snow to wash it down."

New England's rural roads ran past farmers' houses. The compact New England town plan of the seventeenth century, with its houses gathered around a central commons and its fields off in the distance, had given way to more dispersed dwelling places, as the officers discovered. "After that we proceeded about one hundred yards, when a man came out of a house and said those words to Captain Brown, 'What do you think will become of you now?' which startled us a good deal, thinking we were betrayed." By now the hungry, tired, and anxious spies were imagining all kinds of specters emerging from the dark. A later account of a passage through the same part of the country described how "each lifeless Trunk, with its shatterd Limbs, appeard an Armed Enymie." Brown and DeBerniere were afraid of more solidly shaped enemies. "We resolved to push on at all hazards, but expected to be attacked on the Causeway; however we met nobody there, so began to think it was resolved to stop us in Sudbury, which town we entered when we passed the Causeway." Sudbury lay along the Boston Post Road, the main thoroughfare from New Haven, Connecticut, to Boston, but in the snowstorm it is a wonder that the two men could find the road at all.[39]

Worse was to come. "About a quarter of a mile in the town we met three or four horsemen, from whom we expected a few shot, when we came nigh they opened to the right and left and quite crossed the road, however they let us pass through them without taking any notice, their opening being only chance; but our apprehensions made us interpret everything against us. At last we arrived at our friend Jones's again, very much fatigued, after walking thirty two miles between two o'clock and half after ten at night, through a road that every step we sunk up to the ankles, and it blowing and drifting snow all the way. Jones said he was glad to see us back, as he was sure we should meet with ill usage in that part of the country, as they had been watching for us sometime." The two officers, "much fatigued, struggled up the stairs and to fitful slumber," aided by "a bottle of mulled Madeira wine."

The spies' thoughts had turned to the return trip; no stopping now to gather information or sketch the lay of the land. "The next morning after breakfast, we set off for Boston. Jones shewed us a road that took us a quarter of a mile below Watertown bridge, as we did not choose to go through that town. We arrived at Boston about 12 o'clock, and met General Gage and General Haldiman [Gage's second-in-command], with their aides-de-camp, walking out on the Neck, they did not know us until we discovered ourselves; we besides met several officers of our acquaintance who did not know us," so much had the adventure changed the appearance of the two spies.

DeBerniere closed with the denouement of the venture: "A few days after our return, Mr[.] Barnes came to town from Marlborough, and told us, immediately on our quitting the town, the committee of correspondence came to his house and demanded us; he told them we were gone; they then searched his house from top to bottom, looked under the beds and in their cellars, and when they found we were gone, they told him if they had caught us in his house, they would have pulled it about his ears. . . . They then sent horsemen after us, every road; but as we had the start of them, and the weather being so very bad, they either did not overtake us, or missed us. Mr[.] Barnes told them we were not officers, but relations of his wife's [Christian Goldthwait] from Penobscot, and were going to Lancaster; that, perhaps, might have deceived them."

Had Brown and DeBerniere traveled north, toward Salem, instead of west, they would have found the same unrest stirring the towns and the countryside. The first-responders among the militia, the minutemen, patrolled the roads, and the few loyalists brave or foolhardy enough to remain in their homes and businesses were unceasingly harassed as enemies of the people. Brown and DeBerniere's report joined others of similar nature in Gage's hands. For example, one from February 21st reported that "the gun carriages that are making at Charles Town is by one Kinney, a wheelwright but making principally wheels for them, at present, many have been carted through Cambridge, tis said for Worcester." Another memo from spies counted "thirty-eight field pieces and nineteen companys of artillery most of which are at Worcester, a few at Concord and a few at Watertown." Other spies—possibly Samuel Porter, a loyalist, or John Sargent, a merchant and William Browne's brother-in-law (both signers of the address welcoming Gage, who undoubtedly had talked with him when he had his headquarters in Danvers)—were watching Marblehead and Salem, and their messages alarmed Gage. "Gun carriages making at Salem. Twelve pieces of brass cannon mounted are at Salem and lodged near the North River, on the back of the town." In addition, "there are eight field pieces in an old store, or barn, near the landing place at Salem, they are to be removed in a few days, the seizure of them would greatly disconcert their schemes." Gage endorsed the back of the message, writing "Intelligence, February 24, 1775."[40]

three

Leslie's Retreat

On February 28, 1856, Charles Moses Endicott was sixty-three years old, the eldest of the eighth generation of Endicotts in Essex County, when he delivered a talk on the Salem raid to his fellow members of the Essex Institute. A seared veteran of the spice trade in Sumatra (on one occasion angry locals had boarded his ship *Friendship* and tried to kill him and his crew), he had retired from the sea and took on the role of the town's unofficial historian. From other elderly neighbors he had gathered first- and second-hand accounts of the raid. Without his efforts, the remarkable details of that day would have been lost to history. While the passage of time and the toils of old age had thickened the bodies and bent the recollections of his informants, Endicott was a meticulous and dedicated antiquarian. In his hands, the story almost told itself.[1]

To preserve such memories, men like Endicott had founded the Institute. In 1856 it housed the library of the Essex Historical Society (established in 1821) and the collections of the East India Marine Society (chartered in 1799). Plummer House, which was leased by the Institute, was the home of the Salem Athenaeum. When the first *Proceedings of the Essex Institute* and the *Essex Institute Historical Collections* were published, the editors made it clear that "the principal object that the founders of the Essex Historical Society had in view . . . was the collection and preservation of authentic memorials relating to the civil history of the county of Essex . . . and of the eminent men who have resided within its limits." The account of the Salem gunpowder raid clearly fit that agenda, as it was all about the role of eminent men.[2]

The first proceedings, published three years before the regular *Historical Collections* began to appear, included Endicott's "Colonel Leslie's Retreat." In the great hall of the first floor of Plummer House, chilly in the late winter and no doubt clouded by his fellow members' cigar and pipe smoke, Endicott apologized to the gathering: "It is much to be regretted that antiquarian research had not been directed to this affair, before the principal actors in the scene were gathered to their fathers. Before the task was undertaken by me, the twilight of uncertainty had cast its shadows over a large portion of the incidents . . . the following account however is believed to embrace all the principal facts in the case." He nevertheless claimed to present "the most authentic and reliable" recollections. When used with care and affection, for those were the qualities Endicott lavished on his sources, the account is invaluable.[3]

Endicott opened his account with the political crisis following Gage's unhappy sojourn in Salem. A "Second Provincial Congress [of Massachusetts] held its first session at Cambridge from the 1st to the 16th of February [1775], and the collection of stores received immediate attention." As successive presidents of the Provincial Congress, John Hancock, the richest merchant in Boston and (with Samuel Adams) a prime mover of the rebellion, and Joseph Warren, a young doctor from one of the best families in the colony, took a leading role in raising funds and troops. The men would need sustenance: "300 bushels of pease and beans, 20 hogsheads of molasses, 150 quintals of fish, and two chests of carpenters' tools were ordered to be sent to Concord, followed on the 23d by 20 hogsheads of rum. To these was added on the 24th an order for 1,000 lbs. of candles, wooden spoons, two barrels of oil, 1,500 yards of Russian linen, 15 chests of medicine, 20 bushels of oatmeal, 100 hogsheads of salt, six casks of Malaga wine, nine casks of Lisbon wine, and 20 casks of raisins."[4]

Most important, however, were cannons. Coastal New England towns often stored cannons taken from the enemy French by privateers. These were useless on land without caissons (wheeled carriages for each individual cannon) and limbers (the balancing back projection to which could be added a second set of wheels) to move the cannons. Colonial barrel makers and blacksmiths, however, could fashion these. On "February 13th Colonel Robinson was requested to send four brass field-pieces and two mortars to Concord," as well as "10 tons of lead balls, [and] 30 rounds each of cartridges for 15,000 men." These were supplies for an army in the field, not a home guard. Benjamin Church, Gage's spy in the Provincial Congress, had told him about this order, and it was one reason why Gage gave Brown and DeBerniere the instructions he did when he sent them to scout the road to Concord.[5]

Most ominous, in Gage's thinking, were the field pieces. The gunpowder raids on both sides indicated the importance of cannons in eighteenth-century combat. Cannons could effectively block the passage of men over the narrow necks connecting peninsular port towns, like Boston and Salem, to the mainland. Cannons could cause havoc among troops maneuvering in the European fashion. Gage had personal experience that taught him the value of field pieces in battle. Had he not left two light cannons behind in the final advance on the French and Indian encampment at the forks of the Ohio River in 1755, General Braddock's forces might not have been so badly mauled. Had Gage convinced his superiors to use artillery in the assault on the French at Fort Ticonderoga, three years later, the British might not have lost one-fourth of their men. Gage knew that his New England opponents could field more than twice his numbers in battle, over 16,000 men to his fewer than 4,000, fighting on their own ground, from behind New England's many stone fences in what was called Indian fashion. If the rebels deployed cannons, they might actually defeat him. If he could field cannons, he could effectively deny them the advantages of their numbers. Gage had the advantage of navy ships with cannons, which delivered a devastating barrage during the colonial retreat at the Battle of Bunker Hill, but these could only be deployed along the coast.[6]

When Gage learned that Salem craftsmen were making carriages for cannons, he turned to the 64th Regiment of Foot to carry out the raid. The regiment was still stationed on Castle Island, the closest unit to Salem by sea. Keeping the men relatively isolated on the island reduced the chance that they would desert. The men and their officers had already spent time in Salem during Gage's sojourn there. They knew the way from the landing at Marblehead up the road to Salem. They knew about the layout of streets in the town, and how the North River cut off the main business portion of Salem from the foundry, where workers turned bars of iron into tools and other useful shapes, and other structures on the hill above the river. It was thus natural that Gage would turn to the regiment and its commanding officer, Colonel Alexander Leslie, to capture the town's ordinance.

Leslie was born in 1731, the youngest son of a high-ranking family with a rich military tradition that stretched back to the civil wars of the previous century. He entered the army in 1753, in time for service in the French and Indian War, and by 1760 had risen to a lieutenant colonelcy. He and the 64th were quartered in Boston from 1768 to 1769. Gage knew Leslie, and had ordered him to prepare to safeguard the defendants in the Boston Massacre should riots follow their acquittal. When Gage returned to Boston, he discovered that Leslie was quartered there, and the two men found one another's company congenial. In Danvers in the summer of 1774, Gage ordered Leslie and his regiment to bivouac in the town, and the two men might have spent some time in neighboring Salem.[7]

There is one piece of correspondence between Gage and Leslie on January 14, 1775, that offers a tantalizing clue to the range of possibilities that Gage entertained for the raid. He wrote Leslie that he had issued a warrant to the keeper of the provincial stores secured at Castle William to provide Leslie with twenty stands of arms and adequate ammunition, and to put that cargo aboard the customhouse schooner for delivery to the Marblehead customhouse. A stand of arms was a musket, a bayonet, a cartridge box, and anything else a soldier would need to use the weapon. This instruction to Leslie makes little sense if Gage's thinking was solely directed to swift and small-scale gunpowder raids like those on Charleston and Cambridge, adjacent to Boston. For such a mission, Leslie's men would have carried their own muskets and ammunition. What was more, customhouses were hardly safe storage facilities by this time. Why would Gage put arms and ammunition virtually in the hands of the Marblehead militia? If, instead, Gage were thinking about garrisoning Marblehead, the instruction would make perfect sense. Marblehead was on a peninsula, closer to British ports like Bristol and Portsmouth than was Boston. The peninsula could also be easily defended against land attack. Leslie never carried the order out, however, because Gage evidently changed his mind.[8]

If there was a written record of Gage's orders to Leslie to find the Salem cannons after the January 14th letter, it no longer exists. This is not surprising, as Leslie was quartered nearby, and Gage would probably have summoned the colonel and given him his orders verbally. One does not like to conjure

HON. ALEXANDER LESLIE.
Lieut-General & Colonel 9th Reg. of Foot,
born 1731, died 1794.

Colonel Alexander Leslie, by John Kay. Emmet Collection, Miriam and Ira D. Wallach Division of Art, Prints and Photographs, The New York Public Library, Astor, Lenox and Tilden Foundations.

up conversations from the ether of the past, a literary device that belongs to the historical novelist rather than the scholar. Nonetheless, a conversation between the two men must have taken place. Gage was a temperate, almost stolid man, and he would not have raised his voice. Doubtless he undemonstratively told Leslie to figure out the logistics himself, perhaps adding that the HMS *Lively*, part of the fleet blockading Boston Harbor, would be a suitable vessel for transporting the troops. If Leslie raised any objections, they are lost to history. Leslie was proud of his men and, more than likely, looked forward to accomplishing the mission.[9]

Their meeting came sometime after Gage was advised by a loyalist that the militia had stored a substantial number of cannons in Salem. This information would have reached Gage after the beginning of the new year, probably before January 14th. The source of the intelligence about the cannons in Salem is unknown, although many of the patriot party in Salem would later assign blame to Samuel Porter, a Tory lawyer, while others preferred John Sargent, William Browne's brother-in-law. According to Endicott's researches, "most of the cannon had been collected by Colonel David Mason . . . and left with Captain Robert Foster, a 'North Fields' blacksmith, to be put in shape." Richard Skidmore, a Danvers wheelwright, was at work on gun-carriages for the cannons. They were twelve-pounders (the designation refers to the weight of ball the cannon fired) that were landed from colonial ships, generally privateers preying on French merchant vessels during the French and Indian War. Possibly some were prizes taken from the captured vessels during the late conflict. The twelve-pounder was the primary type of cannon in the colonial arsenal and, loaded with ball or canister, could wreck havoc on an enemy. The problem was that the twelve-pounder, whether iron or brass, was a beast (the tube alone weighed over a thousand pounds), hard to move about in the best of times. Now time was short for both the minutemen to secrete the cannons and their carriages, and the British to find and secure them.[10]

Leslie prepared his men for a predawn embarkation. The *Lively* lay at anchor at the long wharf in Boston Harbor and would serve Leslie's purpose. It was smaller than a frigate and somewhat ungainly, but highly seaworthy. The ship was built and launched in 1756 and saw service in the Canadian and Caribbean theaters of the French and Indian War. In the late evening of February 25th, the ship's pilot set a course for Castle Island. As a part of the blockade force, the ship's comings and goings were not unusual. "Parties of townsfolk were in the habit of visiting the fort on a Saturday, and some were lounging about while all this was going on. Fearing an express might be sent to warn Salem in case the troops' errand was suspected, no outsiders were permitted to leave the Island before ten, Monday morning. Parson Stiles mentions that 'the Milkmen who supplied the Castle with milk' were of this number and by his account only fifteen regulars remained behind as garrison."[11]

Gage's plan had the full cooperation of the Royal Navy. He had developed this rapport during his stay in New York City as commander-in-chief of the army in North America, and he relied on the navy for assistance in enforcing the Port Act. There was no joint chiefs of staff and the two services were independent, so cooperation depended to a great degree on the ability of the naval commanders and army generals to work together. At best, these personal ties enabled the British to control a vast coastline with relatively few men and ships. It helped that families sometimes had sons in high-ranking positions in both services. The Howe brothers were an example: Richard was an admiral, and William a general. Their command of the Long Island and New York City campaigns of 1776 ensured that British forces routed the Continental defenders. Gage's third son, William Hall Gage, would command a Royal Navy frigate during the Napoleonic wars and rise to the rank of admiral. Gage could count on the Royal Navy to support his landings and ferry his men.[12]

Gage later reported that Leslie had taken "a detachment" of 400 men. Other observers placed the number at 300. A later history offered the number "140 soldiers," while another estimated "240," and a third abandoned numbers to report "a small detachment." Round numbers are suspect, an indication that someone might be guessing. As a rule of thumb, the more agitated the observer, the higher the number. For this reason, a conservative count is the most reliable. A detachment would have been a part of the regiment. The regiment itself, formed in 1758, would ideally have had a roster of 30 officers (a lieutenant colonel in command, a major, 8 captains of companies, and 20 lieutenants), 20 noncommissioned officers, and about 400 rankers. The 64th, on January 1, 1775, returned (had an official count of) 335 corporals and privates fit for duty, 9 unfit, and 46 wanting (missing from the muster). Similar numbers were returned on the roster for April 1st. Even if Leslie had taken every man, he could not have brought 400, and observers reported that he left men in the Castle William barracks. Thus probably about 250 men of the 64th quietly filed out of the barracks of Castle William and boarded the *Lively*.[13]

The men expected only a day trip, and they were not wearing their great-coats or taking bedrolls. Instead, they wore white shirts and vests, and scarlet coats with the black trim of the regimental colors (uniforms varied from regiment to regiment). They made one final inspection of the condition of their muskets and their socket bayonets, checked again the waterproofing on their cartridge pouches (a ball and gunpowder charge wrapped together in paper), and grumbled and grunted, as all infantry will, about the hour, the mission, and the prospect of many hours at sea.

The infantry carried flintlock smooth-bore muskets, the .75 caliber British land pattern ("Brown Bess") musket. The range of the musket was about two hundred yards, and its accuracy was no more than fifty, so effective fire had to be laid by volley, the men standing in line. The musket's design went through periodic updates improving the firing mechanisms, but on the eve of the Revolutionary War, even in skilled hands the best of them could only fire two or three times a minute. The black powder that propelled the balls released smoke that was so dense that the field of fire soon became clouded, one reason (others being the slow rate of fire and the fouling of the rifled barrel) that more accurate rifled muskets were not widely employed. The requirement that the line face the enemy and discharge the muskets simultaneously imposed great demands of discipline on the men and their officers. Keeping the line intact when enduring the enemy's volleys required a comprehensive and deeply instilled discipline, enforced by the noncommissioned officers who stood at the end of each line. Men who broke ranks faced severe penalties. Often, the opposite behavior of the troops troubled their officers—the men were too eager to go into battle, and in combat they refused to obey orders restraining them.[14]

If the troops met trouble, they knew the drill by heart: march by column, and reform in double line to fire. The commands were always the same, no matter what spot they found themselves in—prime and load to begin the routine, handle cartridge, prime, load the rest of the powder and the ball in the barrel, ramrods out, ramrods back, make ready, present, and fire—until the words had no particular meaning; only their sequence and the cadence mattered. "Aim" was not a part of the drill; the soldier pointed the muzzle in the general direction of the enemy and fired. The musket was the infantryman's constant companion: "In the age of lace ruffles, perukes and brocade, Brown

Bess was a partner whom none could despise. An out-spoke flinty lipped brazen-faced jade, with a habit of looking men straight in the eyes." Yet the men of the 64th knew "even when at its best," their eight-pound Brown Bess might not perform. Hopefully, the march would be uneventful.[15]

The coast of Massachusetts from Boston Neck to the town of Salem is a series of bays, promontories, and necks, running roughly southwest to northeast, not an easy course to chart in the best of weather, and certainly not in the dark of an early winter morning. Then, warmer air from the sea travels over the snowbound coast, and the resulting fog obscures landmarks. A gusty day would raise whitecaps and crosswinds. The ship's pilot had to chart a course through these, first due south to Castle Island, where the 64th was quartered; then east by southeast around the tip of Deer Island; then stand out miles from the shore of Lynn Bay, turning northeast past the tip of Nahant Point; then up Nahant Bay to Marblehead Neck; then steer a half circle around the neck to drop anchor opposite the leeward beaches in the sheltered southwestern portion of Marblehead. Captain Thomas Bishop had taken the *Lively* to Boston in 1774. Having sailed the waters around Boston Bay and the Massachusetts coast for nearly ten months, he carried off his part of the mission with skill and efficiency. He and his crew's role in the raid was one of the many proofs of the Royal Navy's superb seamanship in American waters.[16]

The trip took nine hours, the men cramped together belowdecks on the HMS *Lively*. Its twenty cannons were secured on the open deck above them, but the space belowdecks was still cramped, the insides of the hulls sweated and groaned, the bilges stank, and vermin crawled in every nook and corner, a truly "loathsome and nasty" experience. No one was allowed on deck, lest Paul Revere's spy network discover the troops (though he had already been informed that something was afoot), and in winter waters the men must have been seasick by the time they reached the relative shelter of Marblehead Harbor. Homan's Cove, named for one of the town's leading landowners, was a small crescent of rocky beach about a quarter of a mile from the entrance to Marblehead Harbor, deep enough for the ship to wait out low tide. Once anchor was dropped and the order given to disembark the troops, the sailors would have had to lower boats and row the troops to the beach. With no more than twenty-five or so men fitting in the ship's longboat, there would have been at least ten round trips. The men would then have had to scramble up the path to Front Street and head for the Country Road that led to Salem,

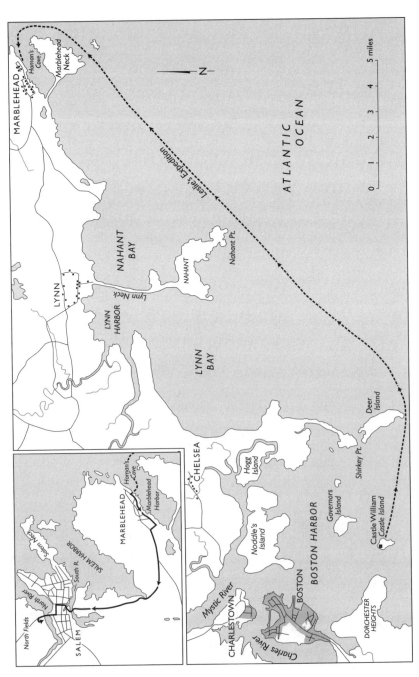

Marblehead to Boston. Map by Bill Nelson.

enter the town itself from the south, cross the Mill Pond Dam's sluice bridge across the South River, traverse the streets to the North River, and, ideally, cross it to reach Foster's forge, where the cannons were allegedly housed.

The men remained belowdecks until the church bells at Marblehead called the townspeople to the afternoon service. Then the crew began to row the longboats containing the soldiers to the shore. There they assembled in column and set off along the edge of Marblehead, up toward Salem. At least they did not have to slog through the snow that slowed Brown and DeBerniere's travels, some forty miles to the west, as coastal Massachusetts has a different weather system from the interior. Undoubtedly shivering in the cold winter wind, the men of the 64th kept step to a fife-and-drum rendition of "Yankee Doodle" (an English army ditty mocking the airs of colonial militia officers). No more than two hours now, and then, if all went well, spiking the cannons and carrying the powder back the way they came, they would be back in their barracks. "A soldier's lot was not a happy one."[17]

Ordinarily, the regimental commander and his second-in-command would have ridden on horseback when the regiment was marching. There is no mention in any of the accounts that Leslie was mounted or that the British had brought mounts. The *Lively* no doubt had, at one time or another, transported mounts for the regiments of dragoons that served in the North American imperial wars and would again serve during the Revolutionary War. Had Leslie been mounted, Salem's locals would surely have added some humorous remarks about his horse: a "hobby-horse" or a "high horse," or the more smutty "mounting a horse" or being "unhorsed." Leslie appears to have walked the ten-mile round trip from the *Lively* to the North River and back again with his men.[18]

Leslie's hope for surprise was forlorn from the start. One supposes that the band did not begin playing until the skirmishers in the vanguard of the column reported civilian figures watching the troops from the town. (Marblehead men were notorious for not attending church.) With the brass buttons of their red-and-white uniforms shining in the mixed sun and clouds, who could have missed a column heading for the road to Salem? By the time that Leslie and his men passed beyond Marblehead, the townspeople all knew about the Regulars.

Major (a courtesy title from the last war and his rank in the militia) John Pedrick was among those townspeople. He had done well for himself in Marblehead since the war, owning three fishing vessels and leasing out

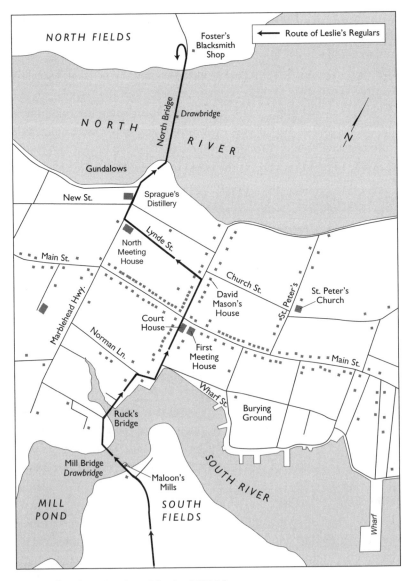

Route of Leslie's Regulars. Map by Bill Nelson.

others (fishermen rarely owned the sloops they sailed on). Pedrick mounted his horse at the meetinghouse in the center of town, spurred over low stone walls in a dash for Salem to warn its minutemen of Leslie's approach, and found himself, embarrassingly, at the rear of Leslie's column marching up the road to Salem. He saw Leslie at the back of the column and hailed him.

Local lore has it that Pedrick, who had served with Leslie in the late war, acted as if nothing were amiss, and the colonel replied with a cordial wave, then ordered his men to step sideways and allow Pedrick to pass.[19]

Leslie's decision to approach the town in an almost ceremonial manner bore something of the aspect of a Sunday military parade, similar to many others the people of eastern Massachusetts witnessed when British troops had served in New England during the French and Indian War. It demonstrated the discipline and purpose of the Regulars and hinted at the dangers of resisting their progress. Marblehead might be a patriot stronghold, but the women and children still found the Regulars a stirring sight. The band was playing a gay tune, and the men were in column, not line, with muskets shouldered. After all, Massachusetts was still part of the British Empire that the Regulars, in theory at least, were defending. Why not a courteous exchange of hellos and waves between Leslie and Pedrick? What was more, Leslie and the 64th had done it all previously, in the summer of 1774. Sunday was not an unusual time for a parade. The soldiers sometimes went to church on the Sabbath, but more often they used it as a day of rest. A more cynical view would say that Gage had intended to take advantage of the church day, when most of the residents would be at prayer. But in these perilous times, men were bringing firearms to church, and it would be far easier for the militiamen to spread word of a British gunpowder raid at a few packed meetinghouses than it would during the week, when the male population was dispersed about the county or at sea.

Pedrick reached Salem to find that his was old news. The town's patriot selectmen had already repaired to Colonel David Mason's home in the center of town and found that Mason was an attentive listener. Many years after the fact, Salem recalled that Mason was "universally esteemed and respected by his fellow townsmen . . . a self made man; one of nature's nobility; courtly and refined in manners and address." Mason had been one of the founders of the Boston artillery company, and he knew that swift action was required.[20]

Mason and Pedrick were experienced soldiers and set about their tasks expeditiously. Pedrick rode off over the bridge connecting Salem town to the North Fields to arouse the rest of Essex County. As Brown and DeBerniere had discovered, the minutemen had fashioned a system of watch and warn based on fast-riding messengers. Mason hurried to the North Church meetinghouse, a block from the bridge over the North River, and informed his fellow congregants of Leslie's approach. "Colonel Mason then flung himself on his horse and galloped to secure the cannon. There were plenty of helpers, even a Quaker, David Boyce, living next door to the church, hitched up his team and rattled over the bridge to lend a hand." Mason again had to cross the bridge, meaning that the draw was still lowered at this time.

Conjuring up this scene proved that Endicott was an able narrator. "In a moment all was bustle, the guns [at the forge over the bridge] being slung as rapidly as possible under the axles of the farmers' oxcarts, and scattered in various directions. Some were drawn three-quarters of a mile to the neighborhood of the Devereux house, on the way to Danvers, and then dragged northwest of the main road up on Buffum's Hill, which was thickly wooded, and bedded in amongst the oak leaves, there being no snow. Some of the gun-carriages were lodged at Gardner's farm in North Salem, others were hurried to Cole's Spring on Orne's Point in the same region. Some were taken by Danvers teams to New Mills and hidden in a gravel pit to the left of the road. Others were taken to Burley's Wood (formerly Lindall's) beyond Danvers Plains."

Endicott also collected memorials of some of the more colorful individuals involved in the gun-running effort. "Skidmore, or Old Skid, as he was generally called, toiled lustily with the rest. He had been at Louisbourg, and his fighting blood was up at the bare thought of his newly fashioned carriages suffering capture. There had been no delay in rallying the workers. Aaron Cheever, in spite of the severe cold, had run, without waiting to pick up his cap, something like a mile to summon a Danvers friend. 'The reg'lars are in Salem,' he panted, as the door opened to his knock, 'after the guns. Tackle up your team with all speed, and help carry them beyond their reach.' So great was their zeal, the last team had rumbled out of sight as the redcoats entered Salem."[21]

The farmers of Salem had something that Leslie's infantry lacked: teams and carts or wagons. Some of the teams were pulled by oxen, reliable but slow. Others (for those who could afford them) were horse drawn. The carts and wagons were essential items for every New England farmer of substance, since the purpose of New England farming was to furnish the towns with food and fuel and, if enough surplus was available, to supply the far-off outposts of the British Atlantic empire. The cannons, not yet mounted on their carriages, could be shifted by hand, but they could not be moved far without wheels and teams. One of the most complained-of grievances by farmers during the Revolutionary War was the confiscation of their carts by the

Continental Army. On the other side, British dragoons were especially adept at making off with the Americans' carts, first filling them with pilfered livestock and other foodstuffs. Eighteenth-century armies in enemy country lived off the land. Without carts, Leslie knew he could not remove the cannons and must have read his orders to mean that he was to destroy the cannons by spiking them (driving a spike into the fuse hole) and carrying off all the gunpowder he could find. The soldiers "carried lanterns, hatchets, pickaxes, spades, handspikes [a tool to lift the tail of a cannon's carriage], and coils of rope." Perhaps Leslie hoped to find the cannons already mounted, and intended to drag them back to Marblehead.[22]

The church bells of Marblehead and Salem sounded the warning of approaching danger, as they had in past years when the enemy French were near or an Indian raid was suspected. The East Church, at the corner of Main Street (later Essex Street) and Hardy Lane, was led by its minister, James Diman. He "blessed his congregation" and went off to find something less spiritual with which to defend the town. Schoolmaster Antipas Stewart stopped in the middle of reading the lesson at St. Peter's, the Anglican church on St. Peter Street, and joined the growing number of Salemites in the street. A local carpenter and his apprentices rushed down to the bridge over the sluice gate on the Mill Pond Dam and just had time to tear up some planks before the head of Leslie's column came into view. Leslie paused to allow his own men to restore the planks, crossed the span, marched up School Street to Lynde Street, and then to the Marblehead Highway and the North Street bridge.[23]

In the meantime, detachments of the regiment had spread out and sped past Derby's wharf on Derby Street, as well as along Main Street, passing the courthouse in which Gage had tried to assemble the General Court and, farther along, back to the Marblehead Highway, where the colonel and the main column had arrived. As they approached, Barnard's congregation spilled out into the street and milled about. One of the militia drummers added his measured beat to the fife and drums of the 64th and the ringing of the church bells. The cacophony must have resembled the musical competition of overzealous high school bands at football halftime, each side trying to drown out the other. Pickering may (or may not) have arrived at the head of a contingent of the Salem militia, and they may (or may not) have assembled on the far (west) side of the North River. Accounts of his whereabouts varied, depending on the source.[24]

Soon Leslie was surrounded by townspeople. Mason had a word with ship captain John Felt, and the burly Felt fell in alongside Leslie, matching him stride for stride as he paced along the street. Felt was a minuteman, though Leslie did not know it. On Leslie's other side, John Sargent, the loyalist brother of William Browne, was whispering in the colonel's ear. They knew one another from Leslie's time in Danvers, and local memory had Sargent waving a handkerchief to attract Leslie's attention at the courthouse, before Sargent joined the milling crowd. Richard Derby Sr. arrived on the scene from his home at the corner of Derby Street and Derby's Lane, as did other selectmen, anxious to know Leslie's purpose, though no doubt already suspecting what it was. The ruse to spread the Regulars over the town had not worked.[25]

William Gavett recalled that his father John had told him how he rushed from church to his home, told his wife that the Regulars had come, and said that she was to keep the children, young William in particular, indoors. John Gavett feared that war between the British Empire and the Massachusetts Bay Colony would begin this day in Salem. Ten-year-old Samuel Gray was in his yard when he heard the drums and fifes playing. Drawn to the music and the pageant, he watched as the regiment passed and reached out to touch Leslie—a pleasant looking, stout man intent on his mission. Gavett, heading in the other direction, must have noticed Gray, now running alongside the troops, and perhaps wondered why his parents had not ordered him indoors. Gavett could not do anything about it, as he was grabbed by the Reverend Barnard and pulled about face. Gavett became part of a small squadron of men that Barnard assembled to talk Leslie out of whatever he had planned.

For his part, Mason, not showing any of the fatigue he must have felt from rushing hither and yon—he was no longer a young man—had seen enough at the courthouse. Both ends of the bridge were still lowered, and he crossed the drawbridge over the North River ahead of the troops. The river actually runs from the southeast to the northwest, at the north end of the old part of town, separating it from the farmlands locals called the North Fields. It was probably Mason who ordered the raising of the drawbridge leaf on the far side of the river, but no one recalled who actually gave the order. It was as if Divine Providence smiled on the town, and Providence saw to it that the bridge's far-side leaf was lifted when Leslie approached. A crowd was waiting for Mason on the far side, a mixture of farm boys and sailors, minutemen arriving from Danvers and other interior towns, and Salem town's own. Mason no doubt was pleased to learn that his efforts had born fruit. The guns were gone.

The river was not fordable, as it was more like an estuary than a river mouth. Illustrations of the confrontation drawn later tend to foreshorten its width. Though the bridge site (now the North Street bridge on Route 114) was the narrowest crossing point in the town, the river was well over 350 feet wide at the bridge site in 1775. The drawbridge had two leaves, each of which could be lowered and raised only from its side of the river. Hence the far leaf, on the west side, could be operated just from that side of the river. By this time, shop boys and sailors had mounted the chains that held the leaf up and were making rude noises and gestures in the direction of the 64th's men.[26]

It was now about four in the afternoon, and in this part of eastern Massachusetts in late February, long shadows would have foretold the coming of darkness. Leslie's mission would be just about impossible in darkness, given that he still had miles to go to return to the *Lively*, lying off Homan's Cove. His situation was serious, but not yet desperate. Still, the wrong move, the wrong order, indeed, even losing control of one of his men, might result in a catastrophe for which he was unprepared.

In real time, events were occurring almost too rapidly for the participants to understand what was going on, much less to control what would happen next. But in a historical account one can stop time, and in this frozen moment it may be appropriate to ask what the people of Salem and the soldiers wanted. Their purposes can be educed from their words and actions up to this point in time. Leslie wanted the bridge down, so he and his men could fulfill their mission. It was a matter of personal honor and of professional duty. Barnard wanted to keep the peace. Sargent wanted to show his loyalty to the crown. Derby and Felt wanted to protect their property from royal seizure. The shipyard workers, the coopers from the distillery, and the fishermen, most of them with little property to lose, wanted to show that they were tough enough—indeed, brave enough—in the face of harm.

But purpose is not the same as motive. For motive, we have little in the way of direct evidence from Leslie, Barnard, Derby, and Felt, and less still from the ordinary people of Salem. One can replace their silence in the record with the fulsome posturing of the politicians on both sides. Whigs like Hancock and the Adams cousins wrote about the danger to liberty. Loyalists like Peter Oliver, the colony's chief justice, warned of disorder. The Whigs stood to gain economically and politically if Parliament and the crown backed away from their attempt to regulate the colonies more closely. The loyalists stood to gain if the protests ended and they could resume the advantages of their close ties with political and economic allies in Britain. Personality mattered as well: the revolutionaries seem to have valued personal autonomy more than the loyalists, and the loyalists were more comfortable with authority. Certainly the differences in personality were in play that late afternoon, as the crisis came to a head.[27]

Gavett's narrative revealed that he had known some of the colonel's men when they had been stationed in Salem. "In the hope of recognizing some one," Gavett "peered at the faces of the redcoats as they swung by." They were in no mood for pleasantries, however, and as they brushed by him, one called out: "Hang it. What are you looking after?" Gavett was looking for someone with whom he could parlay, but the officers were rushing the men to the edge of the water.

Fortunately for everyone, "although so many had gathered, only one of the Patriots had arms; this was an apprentice of Mr. Holman's, who brought a gun and equipments under his cloak." Local reports had a pistol and muskets concealed here and there as well, though pistols were comparatively rare and too expensive for an apprentice; this recollection was probably a later invention. In the growing dark, just about anything might have passed for a pistol butt. In all likelihood, a musket could not have been concealed. Even a fowling piece, the more common firearm a Salem farmer might have had over his mantle, would have stuck out to the soldiers' keenly shifting eyes as they scanned the growing crowd. Salem did not bristle with arms during Leslie's stay, though some accounts had contingents of militia piling out of Beverly to the north, Danvers to the west, and Marblehead to the south to join Salem's own militia. But this much is clear—Leslie did not face armed militia formations drawn up against him during his hours at the bridge.

Local memory reported that "Leslie was properly vexed when he saw the bridge raised and the lads scrambling up by the chains to roost 'like so many hens' atop of the draw. 'Down with that draw,' he commanded, and stamped his foot." Leslie knew that the longer he was stationary, the more likely it was that someone's act would trigger violence. Gage had made it plain that violence was to be avoided and private property protected on these raids. When Leslie's words had no effect, Sargent supposedly exclaimed half unconsciously, "It is all over with them." He meant the Regulars, but someone asked, "What do you mean?" He replied, "They are going after the guns."

Richard Derby had moved closer to Leslie, the crowd parting to let the big man through. Used to having his orders obeyed (his much practiced quarter-deck voice carried for blocks), he thought he might resolve the issue by shouting it down. He did not contribute much to a "peaceful surrender" of either the cannons or the British military contingent. Instead, he just got angry. Cannons? "Find them if you can!" he retorted. "Take them if you can, they will never be surrendered."[28]

Leslie needed a better sight line, and he and his officers walked over to Browne's wharf to see if there was some alternative to the bridge. Local memory had him saying to one of his captains, "You must face about this division and fire upon the people," though that also seems a later invention. Leslie must have realized that the best way to move the crowd back was to have his men advance with fixed bayonets rather than fire. Still, the invention of these words (in an address commemorating the centennial of the raid) afforded the orator at that later time with a chance to credit Felt for his courage. At Leslie's side, Felt followed him onto the wharf. Catching the word "fire," he cried hotly: "Fire, you had better be d—— than fire! You have no right to fire without further orders. If you fire you will all be dead men, for there is a multitude, every man of whom is ready to die in this strife." The story continued that a Quaker, William Northey, was horrified at the thought that bloodshed might begin where he was standing. He whispered to Felt, "Do you know the danger you are in, surrounded by armed troops, and an officer with a drawn sword in his hand?" Less prudent voices drowned out Northey's. "A man sitting on the drawbridge just then piped out, 'Soldiers, red jackets, lobster-coats, cowards, damnation to your government!'" Northey, now shaking with apprehension, cried aloud, "Do not wantonly irritate the troops!" After the Revolution, Northey was a selectman who greeted newly elected president George Washington when he visited Salem: "Friend Washington we are glad to see thee."[29]

Northey's gentle attempts to quiet the situation had no more effect than Derby's bellowing. A local named Josh Ward shouted defiantly, "Fire and be damned." The same words had led to the Boston Massacre, for when the guard turned out on that occasion, someone—not Captain Preston—yelled "Fire," and his men loosed off a volley, killing five in the crowd. Leslie's men were more disciplined, or perhaps they knew about the massacre first hand (they were quartered in Boston when it occurred). Their woolen uniforms were soaked with sweat, and their joints ached with the five-mile march.

Tired, shivering, anxious, they nevertheless held their fire, though the Salem locals did not appreciate the effort self-constraint required. A man Endicott only identified as "Teague," sitting on the far side of the bridge, jeered loudly enough to amuse the other town lowlifes: "I should think you were all fiddlers you shake so!"[30]

Never known for great patience, Leslie was beginning to fume. His men were suffering from the weather, and the catcalls of the locals did not help his mood. He had to get across that river. Local fishermen had beached their dories (open-bottomed rowboats, with as many as four or five sets of oars), pirogues, and scows along both banks. The dories, especially, were sturdy and heavy and wide of beam. The oars for some of the boats might have been left there, though the men were supposed to take the oars with them to prevent theft (like taking the keys to the car). "The tide was low and three gondolas [scows] lay aground on the east or near side of the bridge, one belonging to Captain Felt." No sooner had Leslie seen the vessels and ordered his men to board them than Felt ordered them scuttled with axes.

The wharf stood next to a distillery (on the east side of the bridge) whose workers were familiar with barrel making. They joined Felt and some bystanders, including Joseph Whicher, a foreman at Sprague's distillery, to deal with the threat. Each boat could have transported two dozen soldiers across the river, and might even have doubled as transport for the cannons (for the foundry was uphill from the river, and the cannons could have been hauled down to the boats). "James Barr scuttled his own boat, no less than twenty soldiers jumping into the boat while he was busily engaged." While Barr was wielding his axe, Ralph Wormsted of Marblehead held off the soldiers with a cudgel, swinging it about him like a man possessed. Whicher turned to the boarding party and bared his breast, "daring the soldiers to use their bayonets," for which he suffered "a slight scratch." In later years, so locals said, Whicher happily displayed the scar to any who would listen to his story. Some of Leslie's men loaded and primed their muskets. The scene had grown so ugly that Gray and the other boys "ran and lay under the fish-flakes which covered the south shore from the bridge almost to Conant Street. Here they nearly froze, not coming out until after the troops had gone."

Before proceeding to extreme measures, Leslie held a brief council of war with his officers. He then announced to Felt, "I will go over this bridge if I stay here until next autumn," adding, "I will take the two stores on West's wharf as barracks before I'll quit without crossing." "You may wait as long as you please, nobody'll care for that," Felt answered dryly. "By G——, I will not be defeated," cried Leslie. "You must acknowledge that you have been already baffled," responded Felt. He had a good case.

One must imagine Leslie's dilemma, as he saw it. He was a career officer and had explicit orders to find and remove or destroy the cannons. He had not found them. Sargent (or Porter) had told him that they were in the foundry, across the river; hence Leslie's determination to cross. But by now he surely had worked out the fact that his march's purpose had been discovered long before he reached the North River. The colonials had almost certainly hidden the cannons and their carriages where, with what remained of the day, Leslie would never find them. In short, he could not fulfill his orders. He also had orders not to fire on the locals unless fired upon and not to destroy any private property—the same orders that Gage would give to the officers who led the more infamous Concord gunpowder raid on April 19, 1775.[31]

Leslie needed help in resolving his dilemma, and it came from unexpected sources. The locals wanted to avoid bloodshed, and helping Leslie expedite his departure was the best way to accomplish that end. In any case, the stalemate could not go on. Leslie's honor as a gentleman and officer, as well as his explicit orders to cross the bridge and search for the cannons, would not let him withdraw without some face-saving device. He knew that every passing minute brought more militia to the scene on both sides of the river.

With all the suspense of an eighteenth-century drama, the next act opened. "At this stage young Barnard stepped forward, and addressing himself to Leslie, said: 'I desire you will not fire upon these innocent people. Pray restrain your troops from pushing with their bayonets.' 'Who are you, Sir?' asked Leslie, turning short round. 'I am Thomas Barnard, a minister of the Gospel, and my mission is peace. You cannot commit this violation against innocent men, here, on this holy day, without sinning against God and humanity. The blood of every murdered man will cry from the ground for vengeance upon yourself, and the Nation which you represent. Let me entreat you to return.'" Barnard's words, reported seemingly verbatim by Endicott, sound a little formal, almost as if Barnard were finishing his sermon from that afternoon's service. One must credit Endicott with a little literary license here.

Whatever his precise opening words, Barnard's seemed a voice of reason, compared with the sailors and farm boys chanting insults at the Regulars. Sailors, fishermen, and dockworkers had never had much use for the Regulars. Like the Boston gangs that made the riots of 1765 and 1773 so terrifying

Pen and ink detail of *Leslie's Retreat,* by Lewis Jesse Bridgman, before 1930. Used by permission of the Phillips Library at the Peabody Essex Museum.

to the authorities, gangs of workers and sailors in Salem brought a rough edge to street-corner politics, and the appearance of the Regulars had brought out the worst (or the best, if one took a patriot view) of the roughnecks. Fortunately, as events turned out, the rowdies did not engage in their favorite pastimes of throwing rocks and starting fistfights, as they had in Boston when troops arrived there seven years earlier.[32]

An hour and a half had passed and night was fast approaching. A decision of some kind must be reached. After a little pause, Leslie spoke to Felt, as one senior in authority to another. Locals noticed the colonel's "more kindly manner." He hoped that Felt would be thinking along the same lines as he was, looking for a solution to the stalemate. "Have you authority to get the draw lowered?" he asked the portly ship captain. Felt replied, "There is no authority in the case, but there may be some influence." In other words, Felt was assuring Leslie that the locals would defer to the ship captain. Ship captains had great discretion in colonial ports. They could hire or fire crews, and ensure that the trip was a relatively comfortable one (though no eighteenth-century sailing vessel was truly comfortable) or pure hell. The captain made sure that the crew was paid, the ship was sound, and, in the event of an accident, the widow was given her portion of the victim's wages. Some captains also saw to the religious needs of their men. If Felt told the sailors on the bridge to lower the leaf, they would.[33]

Pickering had finally shown up with a contingent of Salem militiamen, and he, Felt, Barnard, and Derby put their heads together. It was as if Leslie were no longer the enemy, but a man in a pickle, and they, wise heads, would help him. They did remind him that the militia had been called out and that he must agree to whatever they suggested. In this manner a conference of equals had replaced a confrontation between soldiers and civilians. Spectators on both sides now watched and listened as the best men reasoned together. For a moment, at least, the popular politics of the insurrection had given way to older, more deferential ways of handling disputes. The old habits of deference had not died with the rise of popular protest; they could be resuscitated when and if needed.

Leslie decided to accede to the offer. He "pledged his word that he would be content peaceably to withdraw if he could but march fifty rods beyond the bridge." A rod was a measure of distance, equal to about sixteen-and-a-half feet, that was used by surveyors. No one offered to provide rods and chains to determine the distance Leslie could march, but it would have been over 275 yards, well beyond the foundry. "Colonel Mason and the other leaders welcomed a way out of the difficulty and urged the people to accept Leslie's proposition, holding his word a sufficient guarantee." Barnard called out, "Lower the leaf," and was greeted with only slightly more respect than the men on the chains gave Leslie. "We don't know you in the business," they replied. "When Felt orders, it will be time enough." Chagrined, Barnard let Felt call out the order, with a voice that could be heard from one end of the bridge to the other.

After a few more words the troops started over the bridge, marching about as far as the present Mason Street, where a "line was markt." They then wheeled about and returned, the fifes, so the story runs, humorously playing "The World Turned Upside Down." Many women who had stood on Well's Hill, east of the road, watching what took place, were now seen waving congratulations to their menfolk. While the troops were wheeling about to return to Marblehead, "a nurse, Sarah Tarrant, called from a neighboring window, 'Go home and tell your Master he has sent you on a fool's errand

and broken the peace of our Sabbath.— What! do you think we were born in the woods to be frightened by owls.'" Endicott embroidered a little here, adding the tale that when a soldier "indignantly" leveled his musket at her, "she cried shrilly, 'Fire, if you have the courage, but I doubt it.'" Marching back to the ship, the soldiers shouldered their muskets. Any ranker who leveled his would have received a curt tongue lashing from one of the eight sergeants dispersed throughout the companies. If an officer noticed, the soldier might face formal discipline, never a laughing matter in the king's army. The story sounds apocryphal. But Endicott trumped it with another: "Not far from there a man named Symonds is said to have stood with his musket at his shoulder ready for use." At the bridge, Barnard watched the 64th form up and begin to depart. He turned to those of his congregation in hearing distance and said, "This is a season for the exercise of prayer," to which they replied "Amen" and exhaled.

It was indeed a season "for thanksgiving," for the confrontation had again resumed the character of a parade. It could have ended very differently. The Beverly militia had finally arrived, having made their way to the west side of the North River, and "before the British left, and a company of militia under Captain Samuel Eppes, with Gideon Foster as second lieutenant and two clergymen in the ranks—Rev. Benjamin Wadsworth and Rev. Nathan Holt— had already marched in from Danvers and taken their stand by the distillery." Both contingents could have assaulted the departing British, but they did not. When the British started on the return march for Marblehead, this company formed across Main Street and fell in behind the British. Just beyond the Mill Pond Dam road, they met the Marblehead minutemen and together they followed the British out of Salem. "Eight companies, almost the entire remaining male population of Marblehead, under Colonel Orne, lay concealed behind houses and fences from there to the shore, meaning to show fight in case the British should offer violence." The Reverend Barnard also trailed behind the retreating column, with Gavett by his side, just to be sure that no one fired a musket in celebration or by mistake. Barnard, a stout man, was breathing heavily. He had done well and meant to see the matter through.

Leslie's retreat was not without incident. He was overtaken on the march back to the ship by a minuteman rider named Benjamin Daland, who told the colonel that the Danvers men had arrived in Salem. It was just as well that Leslie was leaving, Daland said, for now there were more militia in the town than his Regulars "had lice in their hair." These new arrivals, unlike the sailors and apprentices of the town who jeered the Regulars, came armed. Leslie's response was not recorded, though he surely had strong feelings. His face must have been florid with the day's exertion, and perhaps anger, before he was treated to Daland's jibe. Stiffly, he took no notice of it.[34]

Most retreats in military history are undertaken while the combatants are under fire. Whether they are fighting retreats (as in the famous U.S. Marine General Oliver P. Smith's description of the withdrawal from the Chosin Reservoir in North Korea during the first year of the Korean War: "Retreat, hell, we are just advancing in a different direction") or panicked flights from the field, they are times of great danger for the troops, Smith (nicknamed "the professor") had a thorough understanding of military history and knew that very often more casualties are suffered in the retreats than in the battles preceding them. Leslie, too, was aware of this, having seen the slaughter of the stragglers and the wounded retreating Scots at Culloden in 1746, and no doubt his head swiveled from side to side, looking for possible choke points where his men would be especially vulnerable to colonial musketry as he passed through Marblehead.[35]

Leslie had seen first hand the horrific damage that American marksmen, including Indians, could inflict on Regular troops when the troops were in the open and the enemy fired from behind cover. This "Indian way of war" had led to Braddock's disaster in the western Pennsylvania forests in 1755, and officers who had served in the French and Indian War came to respect the peril of such tactics. While a road along stone farm fences might not be as treacherous a terrain as the deep woods, Leslie did not know how many armed colonials there were ahead of him, but he had seen those who trailed his column and rightfully supposed that many more were watching from cover. To the west lay a low ridge; in the setting sun men and cannons could have been deployed there with devastating effect on the retreating column. Leslie exercised a remarkable prudence. He kept his column moving and got his men safe to the *Lively*. In retrospect, he had performed commendably, given all the acts intentional or unintentional that might have led to blood-shed and serious harm to his command. It was dark when the 64th returned to the cove and reembarked on the *Lively*'s longboats. The sailors again had to man the boats and ensure that the troops were safely returned to the ship. In all, soldiers and sailors performed remarkably well.[36]

With the column of redcoats disappearing down the road, the controversy over who did what to whom and who deserved the credit began. Pickering was at the center of it. Where exactly had he been, and when? Had he actually prevented the advance of Leslie's men? Had he mounted the west side of the bridge with forty intrepid militiamen? "With reference to Colonel Pickering and his forty militia men," Endicott recounted that one eyewitness reported that "'there was no embodying of armed men on our [the far] side, and, of course, Colonel Pickering did not perpetrate the shamefully ridiculous manoeuvre of running backwards with his forty men in front of a battalion of regular troops marching in quick time.'" In fact, it was not clear to anyone where Pickering was until he appeared, as if by magic, at the penultimate conference with Leslie. Even that appearance—like Banquo at MacBeth's coronation feast, which was only noticed by MacBeth—was recounted solely by the occasional journalist who invented "the cool defiance of Timothy Pickering and his gallant supporters." Pickering's son Octavius would later claim that Pickering's hand, like an immanent Providence, lay over the entire affair.[37]

Pickering's own claims were boosted by his later service to the revolutionary cause and the new nation. He fought the British in the battles around New York City in 1776, served as adjutant general from 1777 to 1778, and then as quartermaster general until 1785. He was named a delegate to the Constitutional Convention in 1787, representing his new home in Pennsylvania. He would later join Washington's cabinet as Postmaster General (1791–1795) and, briefly, as Secretary of War. Pickering also served as Secretary of State under Washington and Washington's successor, John Adams. On his return to Massachusetts, he was elected to the U.S. Senate. He died, full of years and honors, in Salem in 1829, three days after the fifty-fourth anniversary of Leslie's retreat.

Endicott had known Pickering, but in his account Endicott saw the Reverend Barnard as the leading peacemaker. "When Mr. Barnard heard the colonel say that he would pass the bridge, he addressed him in these words, 'I desire you would not fire on those innocent people' across the river." Endicott supposed that Barnard's ministerial garb and almost scriptural dignity had swayed Leslie. More divine intervention, perhaps, was involved in the meeting of the two men. Endicott stated that Barnard's words were "'I am Thomas Barnard, a minister of the gospel, and my mission is peace.'" From then until Leslie departed Salem, Barnard stayed at Leslie's side, ensuring that the peace was kept.[38]

Captain John Felt had no one to speak for his role as the leading man in these events, but all of the accounts put him at Leslie's side throughout the affair. With Sargent, Barnard, and others claiming close proximity to the colonel, it was a wonder that the tall and heavyset Felt found any space. But local lore records that "just as they were parting, Leslie turned toward Felt and asked, 'Why have you stuck to me so closely?' 'Had your men fired,' Felt answered frankly, ''twas my purpose to have immediately seized and sprung with you into the channel, for I would willingly have drowned myself to have been the death of an Englishman.'" Abijah Nothey, who was the source of his father's story about the affair at the bridge, recalled that for his father, it was all "Felt, Felt, Felt." According to Nothey's recollection of his father's account, Felt could and would have pitched Leslie into the river.[39]

In 1824, Susan Smith proposed her own candidate for the hero of the day: her father, David Mason. "In the mean time my father was busily engaged in securing his guns. . . . After this was done he rode into the street where the troops had halted, and found Col. Leslie conversing with a young tory lawyer, who pointing with his cane in such a direction as he knew must lead him to the bridge." Mason instantly understood Leslie's purpose. "Seeing their manoeuvres he immediately returned to his post and with a number of others conceived measures to defeat their enterprize." From a perch on the bridge, Mason could see everything—the town, the troops, the danger—if he did not intervene decisively. The soldiers "were now coming towards the bridge in full glee while the people in sullen silence stood prepared for them, and the instant Col. Leslie set his foot on the first half of the bridge my father ordered the other half to be drawn up, presenting him a chasm of forty feet." In her account, as in Octavius Pickering's reckoning of his father's role, Mason was everywhere at once. "As all now seemed to be at a stand, not knowing what would next take place, my father mounted a ladder at the top of the draw and addressed Col. Leslie, with whom he was personally acquainted, and advised him to desist." Mason then played his trump card: "There were expresses gone out, and in a few hours there would be a thousand men on the ground, and probably his men would all be cut to pieces, should they once fire upon the people."

Smith reported that at first Leslie was stubborn: "He replied that he had orders to pass the bridge, and he would do it, if it cost him the life of every man he had." Mason's persistence suggested an honorable solution to the colonel: "If he [Mason] would order the bridge to be let down he [Leslie] would give him his word and honor to go over and repass it without molesting any person or property." In Smith's account, Leslie was talking to Mason, not to Pickering, or Derby, or the Reverend Barnard, though how the two men conversed across the forty feet of water was not obvious. "My father then consulted with the people, and advised them to let him pass over, as he had full confidence in Col. Leslie's honor. Accordingly the draw was let down and they marched over ten or twelve rods and returned in the same order and back to Marblehead as rapidly as they could without running."[40]

Many years later, Richard Derby's claim to have played the role of leading man was championed by an admirer of Salem's ship captains: "At the head of the crowd of armed men of Salem stood Captain Richard Derby. He owned eight of the nineteen cannon which had been collected for the use of the Provincial Congress and he had not the slightest notion of surrendering them." Derby's claim was supported by his stentorian vocal chords: "At this juncture, when bloody collision seemed imminent, Captain Richard Derby took command of the situation, and roared across the stream, as if he were on his own quarterdeck: 'Find the cannon if you can. Take them if you can. They will never be surrendered.' "[41]

Suspected villains in Salem also strove to remove any tarnish from their reputations: "As it is reported about this town, much to my injury, that I gave information of certain pieces of artillery, which was the occasion of a Regiment's marching to this place yesterday;—I take this public method of acquainting the good people, that the character of an Informer, is of all characters the most odious to me, that I was in no way instrumental in bringing troops hither, and shall be ready to satisfy any one, who will call upon me, of my innocence. [signed] Salem, Feb. 27, 1775. Andrew Dalgleish." Dalgleish did not add that Porter or Sargent were better candidates as the real culprit. Or perhaps it was Boston's Benjamin Church, a member of the Provincial Congress and the Sons of Liberty, and Gage's most secret and best spy. In any case, Sargent had fled the scene and Porter was lying low. One local ballad ran: "The Tories in the town / Were all put to fright / Some left their houses / And others watched all night. / Prince, he kept close, / John Sargent, he fled, / And Grant was afraid / For to sleep in his bed." Sung at the top of one's voice in the tavern, the patriot jingle must have inspired its audience with mirth and some bravado.[42]

Tavern theatrics to one side, two achievements of lasting importance were established by the Salem men that day. The first was sensory, the second legal. Leslie's men had marched into Salem very much the mailed fist of the king. In column, six abreast, with drum and fife, they expected to overawe the locals. They performed their part in the highly visual ceremony of martial authority. The retreat was orderly, but it presented a very different visual impression. The authority of the people, voluntarily assembled, asserting control over their own space (the road, the town, the river, and the leaf of a drawbridge), had caused the armed might of the empire to turn about and depart without achieving its aims. Moreover, the symbolic importance of the retreat dwarfed its reality. The rest of the British Army was not going anywhere soon. Salem did not declare its independence. But everyone there could see that the old order and its representatives had been replaced, at least for a day, with the people themselves. Add to this the fact that the minutemen arrived many minutes after the affair was settled. This was not a victory of American troops over British troops. It was a victory of citizens claiming their own over the military doing its duty.

Second, the Salem resisters had asserted the most fundamental of all claims to self-government: ownership of their own property. Salem's people had built Salem by the sweat of their brows. The Masons and the Derbys and the Felts made this claim in, for, and by their actions. Had they sat with pen in hand in some library or drawing room, instead of standing at the drawbridge, they might have called on John Locke's much cited *Two Treatises of Government* (1690), a favorite of patriot pamphleteers. Writing in the aftermath of the restoration of the Stuart monarchy in England, Locke defended the concept of private property against unwarranted government intrusion: "God, who hath given the world to men in common, hath also given them reason to make use of it to the best advantage of life, and convenience." Improvement of the commons gave to the individual the right to enjoy the fruits of that labor. "Though the earth, and all inferior creatures, be common to all men, yet every man has a property in his own person: this no body has any right to but himself. The labour of his body, and the work of his hands, we may say, are properly his. Whatsoever then he removes out of the state that nature hath provided, and left it in, he hath mixed his labour with, and joined to it something that is his own, and thereby makes it his property."[43]

Did Locke's theory of private property apply to the cannons? If left there by the French, or taken from the French in Louisbourg or Canada, were they the British Army's spoils of war? Were they left in Salem to help defend it, a kind of lend-lease that the British could rescind? Or did they, like the road and the bridge, belong to the people of Salem? No lawyer argued the case for either side when Gage reclaimed the guns at Charles Town and Cambridge, or when the patriots dismantled the battery on Boston Neck and carried off the pieces. While this may seem an antiquarian tangent, a parallel and larger question loomed around it. Who owned the land that the Salem men and women farmed, and the seas that they fished, and the houses and barns and streets and schools that they built? Did the crown own them, according to the charters of the colony, which clearly stated that the land belonged to the person of the king? Or was Virginia's Thomas Jefferson right when he paraphrased Locke in "A Summary View of the Rights of British America" (1774): the colonists' improvement of the land, turning forest and park into farm and village, gained Americans true title to the land? "Their own blood was spilt in acquiring lands for their settlement, their own fortunes expended in making that settlement effectual; for themselves they fought, for themselves they conquered, and for themselves alone they have right to hold."[44]

The high roads from town to town were called king's highways (a term still in use in much of the Northeast), but they were cleared and kept free of debris by the colonists. One reported conversation throws light on a kind of quasi-legal exchange over ownership of the roads. At one point, exasperated at the turn of events, Leslie cried out, "I am on the King's highway and will not be stopped." "It is not the King's," interposed James Barr, a ship captain whose privateering ventures during the previous war had made him less than enamored of crown authority. "It is a road built by the owners of the lots on the other side, and no King, County or Town has any control over it." "There may be two sides to that," said Leslie. Barr stuck to his point: "Egad! I think it will be the best way for you to conclude the King has nothing to do with it."[45]

Leslie's retreat was a sensation at the time, but, more importantly, those who pondered its meaning would soon have the chance to put their understanding to the test. For it would have the most significant consequences—some intended, others entirely unintended. The patriots recast a military event in political terms: a people numerous and determined to resist the crown, even if not armed, could still, through moral firmness, protect its property from the might of Britain. For the British, a military venture based on faulty operational intelligence, in effect a "bridge too far" for Leslie and his men to reach in time, became a lesson in how not to conduct a raid. They would not make the same mistake again. As events unfolded, however, Gage's troops would make new, and far more portentous, mistakes the next time they sallied forth.

Intended and Unintended Consequences

four

NEWS OF LESLIE'S RETREAT traveled as fast as a horse could carry riders from Salem to the neighboring towns. For New Englanders, it was an important event. Patriots celebrated the version of what had taken place that was sent to New York from Boston by a "self-constituted vigilance committee" composed of Joshua Brackett, Paul Revere, Benjamin Edes, Joseph Ward, Thomas Crafts Jr., and Thomas Chase. Led by Revere, they composed weekly reports to the Sons of Liberty in New York. According to them, the Salem events "terminated with honor to the Americans." At Yale College in New Haven, patriot leader and educator Ezra Stiles recorded his thoughts when he learned about the raid. "Like Leonidas at Thermopylae" [a reference to the three hundred Spartans who held off the invasion of the Persian army in ancient Greece], Stiles wrote in his diary, Pickering and his "brave heroes" had held off the British.[1]

Most of these accounts (such as Stiles's ill-informed celebration of Pickering's role) were not based on eyewitness testimony. Marblehead's people heard the story second hand, as did Danvers's minutemen. They had not been at the bridge. Hearsay rehearsed, performed, pruned, expanded, and reformed the accounts according to the politics of the speaker. Salem patriots particularly delighted in enlarging on their roles over a glass at the local taverns.

New England newspapers featured the event. Printer Samuel Hall's *Essex Gazette*'s account of the retreat appeared on its front page for February 28th. Like all eighteenth-century American newspapers, the *Gazette* did not ordinarily report news. Newspapers were repositories of essays, letters to the editor (often written by the editor), months-old reports of events in Europe and the Caribbean, advertisements, and official government announcements. Newspapers did not have reporters until the early years of the nineteenth century. But this occasion was an exception—the editor and the contributors were eyewitnesses. There was no byline to reveal who wrote the piece on Leslie's retreat. Although Timothy Pickering's son Octavius later claimed it for his father, Timothy himself never admitted it. In all likelihood the author was Hall. His printing office was at the center of the action, and he had already revealed himself as a staunch Whig. By May 1775, he and his partner, his brother Ebenezer, had removed themselves to Cambridge to be closer and of more use to the patriot party. After the British left Boston in 1776, Samuel began a print shop and newspaper there, finding, to his dismay (though it could hardly have been a surprise), that paper and ink were in very short supply and the quality of what he could find was of an inferior grade.[2]

Hall accused the British of violating the Sabbath with the intent of stealing a march on the patriots, but the villain of the piece (and the peace) was John Sargent, William Browne's brother-in-law. Hall had Sargent hailing Leslie by waving a white handkerchief from an upstairs window and telling him about the foundry location of the cannons. Hall snidely called Sargent "the half brother." Sargent did not know that the cannons had been moved, however, with the unintended result of setting the Regulars and the locals on a collision course. Hall's account had Leslie ordering his men to face about and fire into the crowd, which would have occurred had not "one of our townsmen" intervened. Hall did not know that it was Felt, which suggests that Hall either was not an eyewitness to all of the events or was not standing close to Leslie. Given the crowded sightlines, even if Hall were present, he might not have seen who was next to Leslie. Hall then added an aside about the conversation at the bridge. Leslie had said that he was prepared to remain in place all month. "Nobody would care for that," Felt said; either that, or Hall editorialized.

Hall next recounted the episode of the "scuttling" of the dories, calling them "gondolas," a name that bewildered later historians of the event, who changed gondolas into "scows." A gondola (the word is Italian) is a flat-bottomed boat used in shallow canals, most often to ferry people or cargo. In the ill-fated Continental invasion of Canada in the fall of 1775, Benedict Arnold and his troops used two gondolas (*Hancock* and *Schuyler*, named after the richest men in Massachusetts and New York, respectively) to ferry supplies up the St. Lawrence River. A scow is a Dutch coasting or canal vessel used primarily to haul cargo. It, too, has a flat bottom. The Dutch ferried goods around their New Amsterdam colony in scows. Neither a gondola nor a scow has a keel, unlike the fisherman's dories. Hall then had Leslie vowing to cross the bridge, though it cost him and his men their lives—something of an exaggeration, at best, but then, Hall had to rely on informants whose accounts already had two days to bloat. Though Leslie finally negotiated his way across, and some fifty feet more up the road, Hall judged it a "sad rebuff" to British aims.[3]

Squibs repeating the *Essex Gazette*'s account appeared in the *New York (City) Journal* on March 9th, the *Providence (R.I.) Gazette* two days later, and the *(Hartford) Connecticut Journal* on March 15th. Isaiah Thomas's *Massachusetts Spy*, a Whig paper published in Boston, insisted that it had the "true" account, in which Leslie, "a brave, sensible, polite man . . . conducted the affair with a dispatch and propriety" worthy of his character, though it was a fool's errand from start to finish. The piece was short and droll, avoiding prosecution for seditious libel (the offense of scandalizing the government in a publication) by claiming the account was a translation from a classical source, renaming Marblehead and Salem with classical cognates and calling Gage a "Caesar" who was "betrayed by villainous toad eaters at his table." No one was fooled by Thomas's literary invention, and he prudently relocated himself and his paper to Worcester, out of Gage's reach, three days before the battles of Lexington and Concord. He continued his publishing activities in Worcester until his death in 1831. Thomas was one of the founders of the American Antiquarian Society, located in Worcester, a treasure trove for historians of early America.[4]

Timothy Pickering, who had made himself scarce during the heat of the confrontation, swiftly moved to add his own comments to the newspaper reports, implying that he was, in fact, in the thick of things throughout the afternoon. In a contribution to the *Gazette* for March 7, 1775, Pickering repeated that "the townsman [standing next to Leslie, that is, Felt] declared that the colonel, turning to an officer near him," ordered his subordinate to prepare the men to fire. According to another informant, presumably Barnard himself, Leslie had pledged on his honor that no one would be hurt if he were allowed to pass over the bridge and march fifty paces beyond. The distance in paces is far more realistic than "rods" (the term Endicott used), giving Pickering's account some verisimilitude. In fact, Pickering had time to question those who were present, and he contended that everything in the Salem newspaper's report was based on "eye and ear witnesses." If there were errors, these were the inevitable results of the "hurry and alarm" of the event. Never hiding his light under a bushel, Pickering added that he and forty of his militia faced down the British. Octavius later qualified this fiction: "It is sufficient that he and many of his townsmen went to the bridge with promptness and acted with the resolution and prudence demanded by the circumstances."[5]

The tenor of the Whig press accounts was unmistakable: the patriots were firm in the face of British arms, and they would continue to be so. Such firmness must result in the British, like Leslie, retreating. It was dishonorable to think otherwise. The inference was equally clear: stand firm when the British marched out to the next gunpowder raid and the British would back down, for nothing in the Salem episode suggested that the British would simply open fire. Leslie had not fired on the townspeople, whichever of the accounts of his words one believed. Indeed, as the Provincial Congress of the colony wrote to other colonial ad hoc bodies on March 30, 1775, the events at Salem proved that "an army of observation," acting solely on the defensive, could deter British aggression.[6]

Loyalists read the events in a different light. They were quick to respond that Hall had blackened the name of a courageous and prudent officer. According to loyalists Nathaniel Mills and John Hicks's *Massachusetts Gazette*, a Boston Tory newspaper, "the colonel never ordered any part of the troops to fire," nor did he pledge his honor to cross the bridge or die trying, and he was never "prevented from doing his duty" by the crowd. Mills and Hicks "were authorized to say" these comments, presumably by Leslie himself or by Gage. Other loyalist accounts had Leslie simply looking for but unable to find the cannons and so returning empty handed. No mention was made of boats, drawbridges, or foul-mouthed sailors and shop boys. But the loyalist press did not give the retreat much play, for obvious reasons.[7]

Gage read the event differently. Unlike the patriots and the loyalists, who saw a military venture through political lenses, Gage (correctly) viewed the raid and the retreat as the prologue of a military campaign. Though his own report to Lord Dartmouth, dated March 4, 1775, was succinct, he conceded the importance of the failure. He admitted that the intelligence leading to the raid was "a mistake." Believing that a significant number of brass cannons were warehoused in the town, "a detachment of four hundred men, under Lieutenant Colonel Leslie, was sent privately off by water to seize [not destroy] the cannon." "Privately" meant in secrecy. In other words, Gage had not committed the reputation of the British armed forces in the colony to the Salem adventure. "The places [where the cannons] were said to be concealed in were strictly searched, but no artillery could be found, and we have since discovered that there had been only some old ships guns, which had been earlier carried away from Salem some time ago." Leslie had not searched the foundry, his agreement not including any such action. Gage must have swallowed hard before writing the next lines—the reason why it took him nearly two weeks to send off the report. "The people assembled in great numbers, with threats and abuse, but the colonel pursued his orders and returned to Marblehead, where he had first disembarked his detachment." Gage's report was full of inaccuracies about the cannons, though not about the response of the Salem patriots. Whether Gage was covering up his own ineptitude or that of his informants, about whom he promised to tell Dartmouth when "some more favorable opportunity" presented itself, we will never know. Clearly the Salem raid was not that favorable opportunity. But there can be no doubt that the role of Salem's population during the raid preyed on Gage's mind.[8]

An English version of Leslie's adventure in Salem appeared in a newspaper three months later. It bore little resemblance to the facts but a great deal of similarity to Gage's dispatch to Lord Dartmouth; only the date of the dispatch (March 4th) seems to have been changed. The author of the reportage seems to have verified nothing on his own. "We learn by former intelligence from Boston, dated March 2, that on Sunday the 26th of Feb., a detachment of the 64th Regiment, commanded by Lieutenant Colonel Leslie, was sent to bring away some brass cannon, of which they had information: They landed at Marblehead, and marched immediately to Salem; where they were informed by the Officer forward, that he had been where the Cannon were supposed to have been concealed, but had found none."

Much of this was pure fabrication: there was no vanguard, no officer forward of the column, and no search. "The Commanding Officer however having received intelligence that some trucks [the generic word for a wheeled platform] were seen going out of Salem that morning, continued his march [along] the road they were said to have been taken; but coming to a draw-bridge over an Arm of the Sea, he found the people on the opposite side had taken it up to prevent his passage." Again, exactly how this was learned, and who reported on the tracks of the "trucks" or knew that the cargo was the cannons, was not described. It could not be, for it had not occurred. The account may have confused the bridge at the mill pond, whose repair Leslie's men accomplished, with the bridge at the North River. Leslie "desired it might be immediately let down, but was refused, it being a private road, and he had no authority to demand a passage that way." Actually, Leslie declared (correctly) that it was not a road on anyone's private property, but one of the king's highways. "On this he determined to ferry a few men over in a Gondola (which then lay on the bank) as soon as it could be got afloat; the Bostonians discovering this intention, immediately jumped into her; and with axes cut through her bottom."

How a crew of Bostonians managed to arrive on the scene is unclear. There were men from Salem, Danvers, Marblehead, and even Beverly, but not Boston. It may be that to British eyes, all patriot rabble were "Bostonians," or that the editor of the squib, like Benjamin Franklin's satirical Poor Richard, joshed that all Massachusetts towns were suburbs of Boston. "Colo. Leslie seeing this, ordered a party to drive them out of her; some of the people, however, having obstinately refused to quit her, the soldiers were obliged to use force." Pure invention, this, as was the next piece of news: "Upon this a Clergyman complained of the usage the inhabitants were receiving, when Col. Leslie told him, that if the bridge was not immediately let down, they might expect worse treatment." More fiction still: "The Clergyman then prevailed with the Proprietor to let down the bridge, and the Troops marched on, leaving a party in possession of the bridge till they returned, which they soon did, it being dark, hearing nothing more of the trucks they went in search of; they then went back to Marblehead, and embarked on board the transport between eight and nine that night, and returned next day to Boston." English politician and member of Parliament Edmund Burke, in possession of a more factual account, was sympathetic to the colonists' plight, and he took more sober notice of the Salem gunpowder raid: "Thus ended their first expedition, without effect and happily without mischief. Enough appeared to show on what a slender thread the peace of the Empire hung, and that the least exertion of military power would certainly bring things to extremities."[9]

Gage must have realized that the failure of the Salem raid further dimin-ished his reputation at home, but he did not demote or otherwise punish Leslie. Other generals might have tried to shift the blame, but undermining otherwise loyal subordinates was not in Gage's nature. If Leslie were not at fault, and the gunpowder raids remained a necessity, what could Gage do to ensure a better result the next time? Next time loomed in the supposed storage of shot and cannons in Concord. Gage might simply wait out his op-ponents, but that political solution, his first plan, had clearly failed. A le-gal solution—arrest the leading rebels—would only work if he could get his hands on them. Hancock and Samuel Adams had left their Boston homes at the end of March and headed for Lexington (the Hancocks' ancestral home) and Concord, where the Provincial Congress sat. Gage's spies told him where they were. Though he no longer enjoyed the confidence of the countryside, Gage remained unwilling to order anything more than the gunpowder raids. Yet the "nonchalance" and good will he had exhibited as the first British governor of Canada, and the immense patience he had shown in the face of the patriots' provocations, was wearing thin. Four days before Hancock fled, Gage had offered to protect his home and stables from less restrained British soldiers. Two weeks later, Gage ordered the arrest of Hancock on charges of treason, but Hancock had already departed. Gage must have concluded that something drastic needed to be done to reestablish British authority. It was all about the troops being seen and obeyed by the locals, and that meant a full-fledged display of the might of the British Empire.[10]

Already limited by time (as the crisis escalated) and space (as his mobility was reduced to the environs of Boston), Gage's options narrowed even fur-ther after Leslie's retreat. The solution seemed obvious: the next gunpowder raid would be in made in force, one so great that none might resist it. In an account of questionable origin published many years later, Private John Howe (calling himself a spry lad of twenty-two years) claimed to be Gage's spy. After walking to Worcester dressed in workman's clothing early in April, he allegedly convinced the general to go to Concord. The account, however, is almost a word-for-word copy of DeBerniere's journal recounting the Febru-ary reconnaissance. At that time, Brown and DeBerniere had been to Con-cord and reported the comings and goings of the patriots. Based in part on their report, and in part on what Benjamin Church, Gage's informant in the patriot political circle, wrote about Concord, Gage assembled an expedition-ary force of nearly a thousand men and planned another gunpowder raid for

April 19, 1775. The target was the ordnance in Concord, as well as the arrest of John Hancock and Samuel Adams, who had fled in that direction three days earlier. In the week prior to the planned assault, Gage rested his elite troops, the grenadier companies, and wrote secret instructions for each of his regimental commanders. The British columns formed shortly before midnight on the 18th of April, intending to surprise the colonials sleeping twenty miles to the west, but Paul Revere and his spy network were wide awake, and horsemen (including Revere) left before the troops to alert Hancock and Adams and inform the locals that the Regulars were coming.[11]

There is one clue to the impact that the Salem debacle had on Gage's planning. He sent the later expedition by land on the road to Concord, but he ordered the commanders to avoid contact with civilians. He wanted no repeat of the mobbing of the troops by locals and the long negotiations that followed. He told the commanders that civilian lives and property were to be spared. As much as possible in the landscape of towns and farms dotting the route, he wanted the raid to be a military exercise rather than the beginning of a war. But Gage was not the only Briton pondering the meaning of Leslie's retreat, and its influence on the thinking of his men and the minutemen at Lexington would lead to the very consequence he wished to avoid.

Conjure the scene—a crisp, windy, chilly, early April 19th morning—when a hastily formed line of minutemen on Lexington Common (today termed Lexington Green) saw the head of a column of Regulars approaching. The numbers were similar to those in Leslie's Salem incursion, with perhaps fewer than 250 men in the 5th Regiment of Foot, a light infantry formation. Its commander was Major John Pitcairn, an experienced veteran of the wars for empire. Pitcairn's men were the vanguard of nearly 1,000 British infantry, something he knew but the colonists in Lexington did not. The minutemen were commanded by Captain John Parker, a middle-aged farmer who had served alongside the British in the Canadian campaign. He had contracted tuberculosis there, and he was dying from it. Under Parker's direct command were 38 men, all armed, drawn up in a double line. A similar number of other minutemen, most of them armed, were scattered about the Green and in the buildings on it (where some had spent the night drinking and promising to give the British a good going over).

Both commanders knew about Leslie's retreat—everyone in arms that day did. Neither man wanted to be the first to start open hostilities, but, spooked by a report of unidentified riders who warned his men not to proceed,

Pitcairn had ridden to the front of his column and ordered the men to load their weapons before they reached Lexington. Parker's three dozen men were the first of what would become thousands of militia marching toward the scene from towns all over eastern Massachusetts. Parker told them not to fire until and unless they were fired upon, but their muskets were also loaded.[12]

The fate of all of them, and of a nation not yet born, lay neither in Pitcairn's nor Parker's hands. Pitcairn, like Leslie, had returned to the end of the column, ensuring that no one straggled (or deserted). His subordinate, Lieutenant Jesse Adair, rode at the front of the column, and was just now facing a decision. The young Irishman, who had no experience of war, was as eager for battle as Pitcairn was wary. At Lexington Green the road forked, with the left fork leading on to Concord and the right leading away from the soldiers' target. Adair chose the wrong fork, bringing him and his column into view of Parker's men lined up on the Green. What happened next was almost immediately—and remains—one of the most controversial sequences of events in American and British history.

All accounts agree that Adair ordered his men to advance on the Americans, which they did with almost unseemly alacrity, shouting huzzas so loudly that officers' commands were lost in the clamor. Pitcairn, who had turned onto the correct fork, saw what was happening and rode to the scene with other officers, but the confrontation he wanted to avoid and Gage feared had already occurred. Separated by less than a football field's length, armed soldiers and farmers glared at one another. No one knows to this day who fired the first musket. It was not the British, according to their own accounts, nor Parker and his men, according to theirs. In all likelihood it came from within or alongside one of the buildings on the Green, and its effect was irreversible.[13]

The next series of events seems almost accidental: a shot rings out, and the two sides, unsure of what has happened, respond according to their training (or lack thereof), their sense of personal honor, and their discipline (or lack thereof). The explanation lies in the fact that nothing quite like this had happened before; hence there was no precedent for dealing with it. Things that could go wrong accordingly went very wrong, and a march intended to secure cannons and avoid battle did exactly the opposite. Adair's men fired a volley (scattering all but a few of Parker's men and the spectators), reloaded and fired again, then launched a bayonet charge. Parker ordered his men to disperse. Two of Parker's men died on the spot; others were mortally wounded and died on their own doorsteps, in front of their horrified families.

The British troops were near to running amok when their senior officers arrived and managed to regain a certain degree of order. They called for the drummers to beat the assembly, and the troops responded. Leaving the bodies of the militia men behind them, they reformed and marched on toward Concord. The affair at Lexington Green was an accident, a concatenation of errors and misunderstandings.

No one who writes narrative history can ignore the importance of contingency, where the outcome of an event is not predetermined. One leading recent account of the affray on Lexington Green finds that the day was the result of a "complex sequence of contingencies, shaped by the interplay of individual choices and collective effort within a social frame." It could have turned out differently. Choices made by people who have no way of knowing the effects that their various choices will have discover unexpected consequences when they are brought together. Thus contingency is the historian's synonym for chance, where many choices that almost pass unnoticed come together and tip the scales of history, turning a shouting match into a pitched battle or a protest into a rebellion. Of course, the narrative historian has an advantage over the historical actor: hindsight, in seeing what the actor could not and knowing the consequences of choice, when all the little choices reach the boiling point. But hindsight is not the same as causal analysis.[14]

Recounting the events at Lexington as if they were dependent on a combination of pure chance and repeated individual missteps wrongly omits Leslie's retreat as a factor in the calculations. Reinsert the Salem gunpowder raid's outcome in the actors' thoughts and the actors' choices make a lot more sense. Parker could not have believed that his paltry contingent would deter the British column, yet he ordered his men to stand their ground as the British turned toward him. During his wartime service in Canada, Parker had seen what happened when an inferior force stood its ground in an open field against a superior force. As a military tactic it was lunacy. He should have ordered his men to find cover. The only sense his conduct made was if Parker was thinking in terms of Leslie's retreat. It had worked for Pickering, he may have thought—Pickering and the Salem militia having (inaccurately) dominated the post–February 26th accounts—and Mason, and Derby, and it would work again.

Adair and the 5th light infantry could not have missed hearing something of the stories the men and officers of the 64th endlessly told about what had happened and what they should have done that day. These stories must have had an edge to them, for the officers and men of the 64th had backed down in the face of farmers and townspeople. No matter that Leslie had ordered the retreat; it must have been galling to obey him. Officers in the Boston garrison were "less inclined to restraint" than Leslie's were. William Glanville Evelyn, a captain in the King's Own Regiment, hoped that "we will shortly receive such orders as will authorize us to scourge the rebellion with rods of iron." Major Pitcairn, in characteristically terse fashion, put the matter more bluntly. He and his men were "most willing to give the people here a severe chastizement." Adair and his men would have decided that they would not back down, and in fact they relished the idea of teaching the locals the lesson that the more timorous 64th had not. Hence this time the British were shouting catcalls: "Damn you, ye rebels, disperse . . . or we will fire."[15]

We have little direct evidence of any of the thinking on either side at this moment, but Leslie's retreat was the most important proximate event in the planning of the Concord gunpowder raid from Gage's perspective and, in the patriot camp, it was widely reported and celebrated. Putting Leslie's retreat back into the equation of Lexington Green changes the conduct of the chief actors by providing motive and expectation. Adair did not make the mistake of an overeager and hasty subaltern, but took a calculated risk that a swift advance of his men to Lexington Green in line of battle would accomplish what Leslie's relatively measured march into Salem in column had not—overawe the locals. If his calculations were correct, at Adair's approach Parker and his men would do what they in fact did after Adair's men fired their weapons—run. Parker, in contrast, knew that the firmness of the Salem men, particularly older men like Derby, Felt, and Mason (all of whom, like Parker, were physically imposing, well known, and much respected by their neighbors), had caused the British to stop and reconsider their march, and believed his militia would do the same. Both Adair and Parker relied on the lessons of Leslie's retreat, but drew entirely different suppositions from that event.

When the British reached Concord, there was no repeat of Lexington. Colonel Francis Smith saw to that: no cursing, no huzzas, no forming of firing lines. The British fanned out and searched, discovering three cannons only partially hidden. The rest had been safely spirited away. The morning passed, sometimes with cursing, more often with a kind of embarrassed civility. No one was trying to give offense to the soldiers, but no one, save one loyalist freed from the town jail, offered to help. As time passed, the heavy woolen coats of the soldiers had become even heavier; the high boots seemed to be glued to their feet. They were hungry and, even more importantly, dehydrated. Ordered to pay for what they ate and drank, they found the locals to be sullen providers. The search was taking too long.

By early afternoon companies of militia had surrounded the town and lay in wait along the road back to Boston. Still, no one fired a weapon. The lesson of Salem was still in the minds of the militia commanders: a highly visible and stout display of determination, but no violence, not until the British fired first. They expected the British to back down, and it looked as though, this time, the strategy would work. Once again it was a confrontation across a bridge, in this instance with colonial militia on one side—Colonel James Barrett of Concord in the van, marching in two loose lines down the hill toward the bridge—and the British light infantry on the other side. One cannot know if Salem was a factor in Barrett's thinking, but from his actions one can deduce that he intended a show of will more than of force. The numbers were similar to Salem, eerily so. None of the existing accounts mentioned Leslie's retreat as the model, but the circumstances were the same. Jammed together in a small space and ordered to form a complex massed formation, the British firing discipline failed, and soldiers discharged their weapons. The British officer in charge, Captain Walter Laurie, had not given the order to fire, but he had ordered the men into a formation designed to produce a dense volley—a formation for firing. The colonials returned the fire, with greater accuracy than the British.

The next ten hours were an agony for the British, retreating back along the road to Boston under intermittent fire from a steadily increasing number of militiamen, with the British columns unprotected, while the militia discharged their weapons from the cover of farm fences, outbuildings, and trees. Only the timely arrival of British reinforcements outside of Lexington permitted the original column to fall back on British positions around Boston. The butcher's bill was not as high as it might have been. Gage reported 272 wounded and dead. A count of the militia casualties was not as precise, but 94 were dead, wounded, or missing in action. One, Benjamin Pierce, was from Salem.[16]

The 10th Regiment of Foot had marched to Concord, with DeBerniere duly recording the events of the day, but Leslie and the 64th were not in the order of march that morning. Had he, instead of Pitcairn, been in command of the light infantry's vanguard, or, instead of Colonel Smith, been in charge of the entire operation, he might have seen the danger before it became irreversible. If Thomas Barnard, instead of Jonas Clarke, were the minister at Lexington, he might have had the temerity to walk toward the British and cool tempers long enough for the British senior officers to arrive and withdraw the vanguard. So many "might haves" cannot change what happened, but contemplating the hypothetical enables us to see what did happen in clearer perspective.[17]

What if Leslie had found cannons at Salem and carried them away or destroyed them? Perhaps Gage would not then have committed so large a portion of his entire force to the Concord raid. Adair would not have been quite so bold, knowing the limitation of his resources. Had shots not been fired and men not died at Lexington, the confrontation at Concord, whether or not the British found the ordnance there, would not have ended with a full-dress fighting retreat. There would have been neither need nor incentive for New Englanders to besiege Boston, or for Gage to assault the colonial position on Breed's Hill, or for the Continental Congress to order preparations for the invasion of Canada and the creation of a Continental Army. Beyond the middle of 1775, when all of these events had occurred, alternative historical vision blurs. But if one does not assume that the independence movement was irresistible and independence inevitable, then a different ending to the Salem raid might have resulted in a very different outcome to the protests of 1774 and 1775. Accommodation might have been possible, along the lines that moderates at the Continental Congress in Philadelphia proposed. But after Lexington and Concord, moderation ceased to be an option.[18]

Hypotheticals to one side, the day's work for the soldiers and the minutemen repeated a crucial portion of the Salem raid. The British columns had marched into Lexington and retreated from Concord. But the symbolism of their coming and going was different this time. The dead and the dying littered the road and the fields. The lesson of Salem had been replaced by the lessons of Lexington and Concord. The colonists had now learned that resistance came at a higher price. The British realized, again, that the mere presence of the military would not compel obedience. The colonists would not disperse when shots were fired or cower when a few of them fell.

The road to the Revolution had run through Salem on February 26th, but only one Salem minuteman fell on the road to Concord, the unfortunate Benjamin Pierce. Salem was warned about the shooting on Lexington Green by eight a.m., riders carrying the word to Pickering. But Pickering dawdled—calling meetings, weighing options, gathering up three hundred men and marching them to intercept the British with three stops to refresh Pickering's thirst—and his glue-footedness left them watching from a hillside as the retreating British entered Cambridge. Had he engaged the Regulars, he might have earned the reputation for heroism that the newspapers had invented for him at Salem. As usual, Pickering had an array of excuses, ending with the Provincial Congress's instructions that he not attack, but his disinclination to join the battle was the subject of much criticism. In particular, the commander of the Danvers militia that did intercept the British, and lost seven men, was not pleased with Pickering's performance.[19]

Richard Derby Sr. was a member of the Second Massachusetts Provincial Congress, and when it met at Concord on the 22nd of April, three days after the British had retreated from the town, he proposed that his son carry the full account of "the transactions of the troops under General Gage in the route to and from Concord" to England in his schooner *Quero*. The Congress agreed, with Richard Jr. ordered to fit the ship out, and John Derby (another son of Richard Sr.) to command it. The *Quero* departed on the 29th, three days after Gage sent his own dispatches, but Derby's ship reached London on May 27th, two weeks before Gage's report. For a time newspapers in the imperial capital decried a British assault on helpless colonial townspeople, while the government wondered what had happened.[20]

When the schooner *Quero* won the race to London to present the Massachusetts side of the story of Lexington and Concord, dodging the Royal Navy blockade in the process, Lord Dartmouth was at first nonplused. On May 30th, he released a statement: "It is proper to inform the public that no advices have yet been received in the American department of any event." Undoubtedly he was furious that Gage's dispatch on the navy port ship *Sukey* was still somewhere at sea. London newspaper accounts of Lexington and Concord could not decide if the British had been defeated or routed. Derby, sought by the ministry, had quietly departed London for Falmouth and the *Quero*, and he sailed uneventfully back to Salem, arriving on July 19th. Opinion in the capital soon turned, however. The British people united behind the war effort. A faith in the parliamentary system, a nascent patriotism that did not see the reasons why the colonists would resist Parliament, and an effective propaganda campaign (in the first years of the war) by Lord North's ministry rallied the people of Britain around the sacrifices that the conflict entailed—at least for the present.[21]

In the wake of the British retreat from Concord, the New England militia continued to mass, confining the British troops to the city of Boston. On June 17, 1775, Gage decided to break the encirclement and, with it, the back of the rebellion. First, he determined to breach the colonial positions on a series of hills that formed the headland behind the town of Charlestown, across the Charles River from Boston. Three hills, little more than mound-shaped elevations—Moulton's Hill, Breed's Hill, and Bunker Hill—were occupied by over 3,000 colonists. Lookouts on the HMS *Lively* patrolling the shore of the promontory spotted the colonists entrenching the hills. General William Howe, sent in May to serve as Gage's second-in-command, urged a frontal assault. Henry Clinton, who arrived with Howe and John Burgoyne to stiffen Gage's martial resolve, pleaded for a flanking attack at the rear of the colonists' position, on the narrow neck of land leading from the headland to the mainland. Gage wavered, but Howe was the senior advisor and his plan won the day. It took hours for Howe to assemble his men, and the colonists used the respite to reinforce themselves, including bringing six cannons into position. Howe's 2,000 men could not break through the colonial lines despite two attacks, with the Regulars marching abreast as if on parade. A third charge carried the position and forced the colonists to retreat, but the British dead and wounded littered the landscape. In all, the British losses numbered over 225 dead and 825 wounded, including many of the officers (like Major Pitcairn, who led the charges). The colonists had lost one-third as many, including their commander, Joseph Warren. In three hours—from the landings at three p.m. to the last musket and cannon volleys (at the neck of land)—it was over. Clinton was reported to lament that "a few more victories like this would have put a short end to the British dominion in America." Gage, however, had the final say. In a letter to Lord Barrington, a friend who served as secretary to the army, Gage conceded what he had hitherto denied in public, and perhaps to himself as well: "These people show a spirit and conduct against us they never showed against the French, and everybody has judged of them from their former appearance and behavior . . . in the [French and Indian] war; which has led many into great mistakes. They are now spirited up by a rage and enthusiasm as great as ever people were possessed of." Only Britain's employment of "a great army" could subdue such a people. Whose mistakes Gage meant, in light of his letter about the "mistake" that led to Leslie's retreat, one can only surmise.[22]

Gage had not wanted any of this, no more than did Lord Dartmouth. As loyalist Peter Oliver, formerly the chief justice of the colony, wrote from the safety of exile in England, Gage had tried assiduously to avoid bloodshed. Even the most patriotic of the revolutionaries recognized this. John Trumbull, a Yale-trained man of letters and practicing lawyer, set it to verse. Gage planned the Concord raid, "But peaceable, without harm / The men of Concord to disarm / Or, if resisting, to annoy / and every magazine destroy." Despite the fighting at Lexington and Concord, Gage would have preferred a legal and political solution, rather than a military one, according to an anonymous Massachusetts rhymester who had Gage supposedly saying to the rebels: "But every one that will lay down / His hanger bright and musket brown / shall not be beat, nor bruised, nor banged." Of course, by this time, peace was a forlorn dream.[23]

The last moment of peace, Leslie's retreat, was still lurking in the corners of the patriots' and the loyalists' minds, however, still a might-have-been even after the sheer brutality of Bunker Hill. A striking clue to the impact of the events at Salem came from Trumbull's pen. In August, after the battles of Concord and Bunker Hill had proved that the colonists could hold their own against the Regulars, Trumbull viewed the worsening crisis in light of the Salem raid. His "McFingal: A Modern Epic Poem" is written in mock-heroic rhyming verse, akin to a popular contemporary Scottish collection of *The Poems of Ossian* (1761) by James Macpherson. The poem "Fingal" was one of the *Ossian* poems, published separately in 1762 and hugely popular at the time. Trumbull's alter ego in his own poem is McFingal, a Scottish-born loyalist of the gentry class, and the account is part of a much longer poem.

> And who believes, you will not run?
> You're cowards every mother's son
> And if you offer to deny,
> We've witnesses to prove it by . . .
> So in one ship was Leslie bold
> Crammed with 300 men in hold.
> To Marblehead in dead of night
> The cautious vessel winged her flight,
> And—now the Sabbath's silent day
> Called all your Yankees off to pray—
> Forth from its hollow womb pour'd hast'ly

The Myrmidons of Colonel Leslie,
Through Salem straight without delay
This bold battalion took its way,—
March'd o'er a bridge in open sight
Of several Yankees armed for fight,—
Then, without loss of time or men,
Veered round fur Boston back again,
And found so well their projects thrive
That every soul got home alive.[24]

The last line is the key: no one died at Salem. Trumbull skipped over the bloodletting at Lexington, Concord, and Bunker Hill to imply that the colonists could have won their independence without the loss of life. That was the lesson of Leslie's retreat, a lesson lost not so much because it was forgotten, but because both sides had read it in opposite ways.

Salem did not play an essential military role in the Revolutionary War. Salem men patrolled the coast and manned swivel cannons to keep British sloops at bay, but the townspeople soon decided on a more passive course of action. The town paid for chains to be run across the harbor and ship hulks to be sunk in it, to prevent the British from landing. The next year, the town constructed batteries, with cannons that looked out to sea but rarely fired anything but warnings. Few Salem men took part in the Battle of Bunker Hill. The town never met its quota for men to keep the British bottled up in Boston, and when the British left, Salem sent just a few men to join Washington and the Continental Army in New York. Only Pickering found steady work with the Continentals, accepting Washington's offer of the position of adjutant general at the start of 1777. At sea, Salem men were more active, contributing their part to the privateering business. Although the warehouses on the Derby Street wharf were soon bulging with the spoils of privateering, it was not profitable for most (some of whom ended up in British prisons). Soon Salem was feeling the pinch of scarce food, fuel, and funds.[25]

Prudently, after Lexington and Concord, some Salem notables suspected of loyalist leanings publically renounced their adherence to the crown. Led by Francis Cabot, Ebenezer Putnam, and William Pickman, on May 30, 1775, they declared to the Salem Committee of Safety that their earlier support for Hutchinson had "given great offense to the country," and "now to our sorrow we find ourselves very much mistaken." They pledged that "we never intended the offense which this address occasioned" and in future would "promote to the utmost of our power, the liberty, the welfare, and the happiness of our country." According to Richard Derby Sr., this abject apology satisfied the Committee of Safety of the town, and the former Tory apostates were forgiven. Such forgiveness after a public apology was common in New England Puritan congregations, and this instance followed that model.[26]

But those who had not renounced their old allegiance to Britain were not forgiven or forgotten. Many removed to Boston, and, from there, to Halifax, to the home country, or elsewhere in the empire, driven by the patriots' animus. As the anonymous poet laureate of Worcester explained, in his *Gage's Folly*: "Tories shall fall. Each one and all / We value none of those. / Though they trench deep, themselves to keep / Secure from country foes." The fate of many of these once well-to-do men varied. Some, like Hutchinson, were well cared for in England. Others there, according to Joseph Galloway, were "laboring under the want of means to subsist themselves . . . many, through the prospect of want, have died of broken hearts, and others have been driven, by their extreme distress, into insanity."[27]

Andrew Dalgleish never did convince his neighbors of his patriotism, despite signing the apology of May 30, 1775. He left the state of Massachusetts and died in Glasgow, Scotland. The Pynchons, Ornes, and Holyokes fled to Nantucket, safe under the guns of the Royal Navy, hoping perhaps that when the fighting was over, they would be forgiven and allowed to return. The Banishment Act of 1778, "an Act to prevent the return to this state of certain persons therein named and others who have left this state or either of the United States, and joined the enemies thereof . . . manifesting an inimical disposition to the said states, and a design, to aid and abet the enemies thereof in their wicked purposes," foreclosed that hope for some. The act named 308 loyalists, notably former governor Thomas Hutchinson and his brother-in-law, Peter Oliver, as well as four men from Salem: John Sargent, Samuel Porter, William Browne, and Benjamin Pickman. The Confiscation Act of 1779 stripped these men of their estates (though their wives were allowed to remain and retain their personal belongings, as well as what they brought to the marriage). In the end, however, only a few named in the Banishment Act were unable to return. Samuel Porter died in London in 1798, and John Sargent in Nova Scotia. William Browne had to rest content with the governorship of the royal colony of Bermuda. Samuel Curwen, by contrast, did return in 1784 after living in England for many years, as did Benjamin Pickman, a year later. Timothy Pickering argued for the repatriation of his former Salem townsmen. They had been valuable members of the prewar community, and the new nation would benefit from their abilities, he thought.[28]

Leslie was not blamed or censured for his decision to retreat from Salem after the gunpowder raid. Moreover, he was elevated to brigadier general in time for the New York City campaign of 1776, and he served with distinction throughout the remainder of the Revolutionary War. In the southern campaign of that war, from the siege of Charleston in 1780 through the march of Lord Cornwallis's men to Yorktown, Leslie held the rank of major general; after the war, he was named a lieutenant general. He died in 1794, attempting to suppress a riot outside of Edinburgh.

Gage's career survived the battles of Lexington and Concord and the debacle at Bunker Hill, though he received from Lord Dartmouth the news that he was recalled on September 25th and sailed for England on October 11, 1775. He spent the rest of the war in England, rewarded for his service with promotion to general, and helped prepare the nation for a French invasion that never came. He died in 1787, in London.[29]

Salem found the return of peace congenial and profitable. Though no longer protected by the Royal Navy, Salem's merchant ships once more sailed the world's oceans. No longer merely a port of departure, the harbor was now a port of call for ships from all over the Atlantic and Pacific. But the really profitable voyages were those that carried men and women from Africa to America, the transatlantic slave trade. Men whose glory had been a fight for freedom became men whose mansions were built with the profits of slave trading. This activity began in the eighteenth century under the auspices of the imperial government, and it continued after the peace. Salem was active in the slave trade; eight of its leading ship captains made more than one voyage with human cargo after 1783, until Congress closed the trade in 1808. In later years, Salem historians denied that the town had taken part in the importation of slaves, but the denial was a self-serving consequence of antebellum New England's growing antipathy to slavery.[30]

The Embargo Act of 1807, the War of 1812, and the end of the slave trade hamstrung Salem's economic prospects. Salem protested against the Embargo Act, and it was rescinded the next year, but English and French ships continued to intercept Salem boats and confiscate cargoes. Salem commissioned forty privateers during the War of 1812, and a few were successful, but the results did not benefit the town as a whole. The town's harbor remained busy, but its commercial activities were eclipsed by other Atlantic port cities, notably New York City. Factories now sat like giant toads on the streets of once-elegant residential neighborhoods, town homes became dormitories for young women from Danvers and Beverly who worked in the mills, and the great merchants were replaced at the pinnacle of society by the millowners.[31]

New England itself had fallen on hard times, its young departing the rocky soils and disappearing farmsteads, moving west along the Erie Canal into New York State, then on to northern Ohio, and finally colonizing the Midwest. Salem sent the 23rd Massachusetts Infantry regiment to fight in the Civil War. Its members served with distinction until the Confederate surrender at Appomattox in 1865, though 218 of the men never returned home. Its travails added to the memories of glories past, particularly of the day when Salem faced down the British Empire.

five   Memorial Exercises

WHEN A READER of history asks, "what did the event mean?" the historian replies with a question, "to whom, where, and when?" Historians know that the meaning of the past is not fixed in the past. It is determined by each generation that looks back at its predecessors. Collective memory of even the most public events depends on by whom, where, and when that meaning is explored.

The American Revolution and the American Civil War are two prime exemplars of the phenomenon of a shifting collective memory. The latter contest, at first highly volatile because of its political implications for Reconstruction, was muted by the efforts of veterans of the war to reconcile. The former, while never so contentious as the battle between "the bloody shirt" of the Unionists and the "lost cause" of the secessionists, in some ways ran deeper. To whom did the revolutionary cause belong? Was it the work of the founding fathers? Or did it belong to the street people and the rural poor of the colonies? With the revolutionaries gone to their rewards, who won this "contest for the memory of the Revolution" depended on who was giving the celebratory oration, writing the patriotic verse, or penning the historical essay.[1]

For the political consequences of the movement for self-government so proudly displayed at the North River bridge were not what Salem's revolutionary leaders, or their descendants, had anticipated. The Endicotts and the Derbys expected that ordinary men would defer to them in the new nation, as they had at the bridge. In effect they, like George Washington, would be honored as the republican fathers of the town. They and their sons would be elected to local and state offices, and listened to when they spoke. In return, they would provide the community with jobs, charity, and moral leadership. But that is not what happened in the new republic. By the beginning of the nineteenth century, men of the people rather than fathers of the towns sought and won the hearts of the voters. Democratic politics had replaced republican order, and the Endicotts and Derbys were left with the shadows of what might have been and with fading memories of former heroism.[2]

In 1875, the grandchildren of the revolutionary generation (like Charles Moses Endicott), who were the last to hear their forebears' voices recite what they remembered, had themselves passed away. The Country Road from Marblehead to Salem had been renamed for the revolutionary war hero Lafayette. Broadened and adorned on both sides by elegant Victorian mansions, it bespoke the wealth of nineteenth-century Salem enterprise. The old North Church meetinghouse was gone, replaced by a Methodist church. The revolutionary past that remained was a collection of words on paper. It was inevitable that fire, storms, structural decay, and changing demography altered the cityscape.

As the physical reminders vanished, the longing for a purer past among the descendants of the maritime elite, a craving for a time when life was lived face to face among people in one's circle, was fostering a kind of ancestor worship. Men whose grandfathers were in fact newcomers to wealth and power began to fantasize that their ancestors and Old Salem were one and the same. As the Industrial Revolution and the flood of immigrants from distant and truly foreign lands transformed the face of the old New England towns, that longing grew in intensity. It could only be slaked by a patriotic history, a history fabricated without its seams and tears, a history that only faintly resembled the past. "Nostalgia for Old New England registered Yankee reaction to disquieting alterations in the texture of life: the acceleration of ethnic, urban, technological and industrial change that a generation experienced across the great divide of the Civil War."[3]

Thus 1875 began an era of self-congratulatory celebration. The centennial of independence neared, and leaders of American industry, education, and politics looked forward to its commemoration at the first World's Fair, in Philadelphia. Reconstruction of the formerly Confederate states was over in all but name, and the troops occupying the South were already leaving. The retreat from Reconstruction was on. Stories of racial atrocities were no longer headlines in the North, as the veterans of the Civil War set about burying the bloody shirt and beginning the long reconciliation with their comrades in butternut and gray. "The emotional yearning for peace reached a climax in the series of centennial celebrations," in the hope that the celebration would "heal old wounds," according to one New York City editor, no doubt a Democrat who did not much care for Reconstruction.[4]

Salem's better sort shared the reflected glory of the Centennial Exposition's pavilions of industry and science rising in Fairmont Park, along the Schuylkill River in Philadelphia. The Massachusetts state building, a rambling combination of Gothic Revival and Shingle styles, did not feature Salem —a mark not of disrespect, but of the diminished importance of the old port town. With the rise of Pacific ports like San Francisco and the completion of the transcontinental railroad, Salem's role in the East India trade, like its part in the Atlantic trade and the slave trade a century earlier, was coming to a close. The "pepper coast" of the East Indies had never been a safe place, even for mariners as savvy and nerveless as the Endicotts. The prospect of profits that once balanced the terrors of unfriendly local rulers had now all but vanished. The panic of 1873 had hit New England hard. Banks in Salem had gone under, unemployment soared, and recovery had not yet come. Over ten thousand companies nationwide would fail in a single year before the depression ended. A kind of quiet desperation must have seeped through the Essex Institute's precincts as donations faltered; even the wealthiest patrons staggered beneath the panic. Something had to be done to remind Salem's people and the world that the Revolution had begun there.[5]

The Salem gunpowder raid had meant a great deal to the people in Massachusetts at the end of February in 1775, including the British. After Lexington, Concord, and Bunker Hill, however, Leslie's retreat became something else—a non-event. As one "Salem Man" ("from his earliest ancestry") wrote to the *Boston Daily Advertiser* after reading Endicott's pamphlet, "There never was any 'Leslie's Retreat.' . . . Colonel Leslie was absolutely bidden welcome by the inhabitants of Salem . . . and he took leave of them simply and at his own pleasure . . . but were it otherwise . . . that would be an affair for the British, and not the American, to celebrate." Endicott had gotten it all wrong in a "mere farce and an absolute travesty of history." Apparently no one in Salem noticed the letter any more than they noticed Endicott's efforts. As the editor of the *Salem Register* put it, a week before the hundredth anniversary of the retreat, "we simply desire to suggest that the event is of importance enough to demand some public recognition of it." Though the editor thought that "every school-boy" should know it, one hundred years after the fact neither the Americans nor the British expressed much interest in Leslie's retreat. A "historian" contributing to the *Salem Post* wondered why "no suitable monument marks the spot where the first armed resistance to British aggression was offered." Surely the city of Salem should do something concrete to mark the gunpowder raid! Mayor Henry Williams's response to this query has not been recorded, but he did go to the trouble of sending printed invitations to the luminaries of the Essex Institute to ensure that they attended the festivities marking the centennial of the raid.[6]

When Salem's leaders decided to make the centennial of the gunpowder raid a city-wide event, another conflict was far more important in people's minds than the uprising of 1775. The Civil War, a war of rebellion that Confederates defended in part by reference to the American Revolution, had to be differentiated from the patriotic events of 1775. Though they did not say so explicitly, the Civil War became a prism through which Salemites viewed and justified the Revolution.

On February 26, 1875, the citizens of Salem commemorated the centennial of Leslie's retreat with a day of parade and oration. The city that was once the jewel of the country's overseas trade had fallen on hard times, but it still had its history to buoy it. It was a gala event. Mayor Williams opened it with a solemn invocation of "this the opening drama of the Revolution." The editor of the published proceedings added his own judgment that "the border line between argument and war was almost exactly drawn through the 26th of February, 1775, by occurrences at Salem." For that day "showed the temper of the people, satisfying those whom it concerned to know, on either side, that they would not flinch in the presence of loaded muskets and naked sword blades."[7]

After the mayor read the proclamation opening the festivities, the crowd cheered, a band played patriotic music, "the national flag was displayed," the bells of the town's churches were rung, and the orations commenced—all in all, an event "successfully and impressively carried out." Miss L. L. A. Very provided the opening ode, whose chorus was "The first shot of freedom today we repeat! / Here's to the memory of Leslie's retreat! / A health to the brave ones of old!" Very, a spinster who spent her adult life taking care of her reclusive poet brother Jones Very, was a poet in her own right, but not a very elegant or elevated one. Instead, it was the pure conventionality of her ode that made it fit the occasion. She brought together the two themes most common in these celebrations: veneration for the revolutionary generation and loyalty to the Union. In these, the past was as alive as the present: "Their footsteps are marching, marching today."[8]

Mayor Williams then offered a short oration. His one-year term was just about over, and after it he vanished from public life. He offered a straightforward historical account, drawn largely from Endicott's, but added to it the untruth that Leslie was court-martialed by Gage. He noted that the North Church meetinghouse had been the site of earlier celebrations of independence and of the founding of Salem.

Williams did not mention the Civil War, but George B. Loring, who followed Williams to the podium, certainly did. Loring was a Boston-born schoolteacher, doctor, and Republican politician, who moved to Salem in 1851 and was serving in the state senate when he spoke to the assembled celebrants. He had attended Harvard College, graduating in 1838, and listened to Ralph Waldo Emerson deliver his famous Divinity School graduation address. Loring must have been impressed, for at the time the most admired public figures of American culture were the great orators. New England had more than its share: Emerson, Daniel Webster, William Ellery Channing, and Edward Everett. A favorite theme of these orators' public addresses was the history of New England and the character of its great men. That was Loring's theme as well.[9]

Loring was not a particularly original thinker, which makes his oration all the more important, for he meant it to resonate with his audience. He spoke their thoughts. He appealed to their feelings, beginning with the case for Salem's critical role in the coming of the Revolution, "a blow struck at a telling moment, a word uttered in a decisive hour, a spark falling where the waiting embers lie"—not the "magnitude" but the "significance" of Leslie's retreat made it noteworthy.[10]

He admitted that Salem's contribution was now all but forgotten: "a casual mention in contemporaneous history, a fleeting paragraph in a newspaper" were all that separated the retreat from "oblivion." But the fires of freedom that had recently burned in the hearts of New Englanders had relit the embers of Salem's past. "Warmed by the memory of the heroism" of that long-past time and by more recent events, the gunpowder raid should never be forgotten. Its lessons of "individual and popular greatness" were as applicable in 1875 as they were in 1775.[11]

Loring shared the racial and regional prejudices of his day. He admired the "Anglo-Saxon" virtues and the "spirit and genius" of the Puritan founders of Salem. Those attributes reappeared in the revolutionary leaders of Salem: "impetuous without being rash, resolute without imprudence, . . . patient, economic, honest." They had not "seceded" from the Church of England, but sought to purify it of its evils, the first of many covert and overt references to the Confederacy. For the Confederacy had betrayed the Anglo-Saxon ideals of liberty that the American Revolution pursued. Salem's courage in the face of Leslie's demands inspired a nation-to-be to unify itself in patriotism, charity, and suffering. The achievement of the Revolution derived from the character of these men, "illustrating the power of free institutions to develop the highest human attributes."[12]

If anyone had missed this second reference to the Civil War, Loring added that "for nearly a hundred years, the high hopes and expectations, the great promises and brilliant fulfillment, the intense and oppressive trials, and the sublime and victorious conflicts, the danger and escapes, the disasters . . . of our nation" had continued. But the spirit of Salem had ensured the "privileges and blessings" of American life. These had made "the country what it is"—and he emphasized the present tense—"the home of the independent citizenship, of social and civil equality." It was no socialist dream, based on "the introduction of ideologists and theorists, and dogmatists" who wanted centralized power, but a triumph for the sacred "rights of property" enshrined in the idea of equality. It was the home of the free, "of Abraham Lincoln, the prophet of the wilderness, the seer of the down-trodden and the oppressed, whose great instincts recognized . . . every throb of the popular heart . . . who passed to a radiant immortality through the crimson gates of the great war for freedom."[13]

Loring's closing passages never mentioned the benefits that New England commerce gained from slavery, as those benefits were of no concern to Loring. Instead, "on these shores, [the founders] enjoyed an opportunity to proclaim the most liberal doctrines, to establish the most liberal institutions," and, in these, "they learned the lesson of civil rights in their town meetings and in their popular assemblies." They defeated the "murderous and blood-thirsty savages" and planted a garden in the wilderness with their own hands. Bear in mind that Loring was not a historian, but the best-selling New England historians of his day were just as racialist as he. The Francis Parkmans and George Bancrofts had no use for Native America or African America. But Loring contrasted Salem, "a community based on freedom and equality," with that in which one person was called "master" and one was called "slave," let the defenders of the South say what they may.[14]

The final speaker of the day was the Reverend Edmund B. Willson. He was the minister of the old North congregation, and thus Barnard's distant successor. Born in 1820, the son of a minister, Willson was educated at Yale and Harvard, took the pulpit of the North Church in 1859, and served as the chaplain of the Massachusetts 24th Volunteer Regiment until illness compelled him to return to Massachusetts in 1863. His eyes had seen the carnage of the Civil War first hand, and his address had a visceral character missing from Loring's boilerplate.[15]

The first half of the address was devoted to the character and contributions of Willson's predecessor, Thomas Barnard, but the second half had an entirely different content. The measured, distant, almost cool tone disappeared, replaced by a fiery timbre, borne of "our late civil war." For when the time of compromise had passed, "every day it became plainer that it was a question affecting the nation's life. Every day it became plainer that it *must* be met." In 1775, as in 1861, as in 1875, and as ever, "the wise student of history reads of men of character under all events. It is only men who have a good cause at heart, and who see the principles involved in the contests . . . who make history." These principles, in turn, were those "which carry human welfare forward, which better human society, and ennoble individual character and . . . equality of rights for all."[16]

Historical memory is a collective endeavor, a series of questions groups of people ask themselves and answer. These cycles of selective memory can be constructive or destructive, and they exist over generations of time. Coming from different places and people, they can collide, combine, and fragment in complicated ways. This was true of Salem's memory of the Revolution in 1875. When Salem notables spoke in public about the gunpowder raid, and about revolution, liberty, and violent resistance to unjust authority, they saw the distant events through the lens of the more recent conflict. That filter was a complex one, for secessionists rested their argument on the precedent of the revolutionaries of 1775. They claimed to fight for their rights and liberty against an unjust Republican regime. There were no Intolerable Acts, not yet, but South Carolina's Fire Eaters anticipated that the Republicans would sooner or later strike at Southern slaveholders' property rights, just as the Salem patriots saw a vast conspiracy against American property rights in the closing of the port of Boston and the acts of 1774 reorganizing Massachusetts's government.[17]

How to praise the boldness of the patriots of 1775 and at the same time disassociate their passion from the secessionists of 1861—that was the challenge that Loring and Willson faced. They handled it ably and cleverly, by ignoring politics, not mentioning sectionalism or slavery, and instead focusing on character and principles. If the fathers of the American Revolution and the defenders of the Union were as alike as the two orators believed, it was in their solemn commitment to the principles of human freedom and equality. For Loring and Willson—as well as, one presumes, for the better part of their audience—Salem's history tied the Revolution and the Civil War together as landmark events in the struggle for human equality. These two men did not see that equality in redistributive terms, that is, in raising up the poor or leveling wealth. They viewed it in terms of citizenship: of voting rights and legal rights. While seeing the Revolutionary War through the magnifying, distorting lens of the Civil War may have been poor history, Loring and Willson had grasped an essential truth. The republic of the revolutionaries was founded on the basic notion of the sovereignty of the people. The Civil War enlarged that notion to include all men.

Loring and Willson did not say that achieving equality was a process that was accomplished at a stroke, not in 1775 any more than in 1875. They were members of a privileged class: allowed to vote, hold property in their own names, sue and be sued in court, serve in government, and pass their estates on to their children. Not everyone in America could do that in 1875. Changes in the law expanding the right to vote to women, ensuring the civil rights of all Americans, and creating a government truly by, for, and of the people lay in the future.

The speakers at the commemorative exercises that day in 1875 might be excused for thinking that revolutionary-era Salem would always be associated with Leslie's retreat and that commemorations of independence would always include Salem, but nothing could be further from the truth. Salem in 1875 was not as different from Salem in 1775 as Salem would be toward the end of the twentieth century. The 1975 commemoration brought only an article in the *Essex Institute Historical Collections* and squibs in various popular almanacs that were cobbled together for the bicentennial celebration of the Revolution.

By the beginning of the new millennium, even that recollection had faded, but the light was not quite out. As of this writing, Leslie's Retreat Restaurant on 96 North Street (more or less where the foundry stood) features revolutionary-era decor and a similarly themed menu, including "Humpty-Dumpty and all the king's men" (egg products), french toast (although "the British never toasted the French"), and other delicacies for the officers and men of the 64th, as well as for hungry tourists. The menu also offers a bit of doggerel on the retreat: "Listen my children and you shall hear . . . / Of Leslie's Retreat, before Paul Revere / On the 19th of April, sure everyone knew, / Of that famous day and glorious year, / But at Salem, not Concord, it is known by but few / That fifty days earlier, are you aware? / First Blood was shed for the red white and blue / and Empires flag felt its first tear."[18]

On North Street, a little beyond and at the foot of the Route 114 overpass, there is a historical marker, a free-standing plaque that reads: "Here, in defiance of King George III, local minutemen hid 17 cannons, and were confronted by 300 British troops under command of Colonel Leslie. The Redcoats were routed, with only Joseph Whicher of Salem being wounded. This was the first open resistance to the King by the colonials, and the first blood shed in America's war for independence." "Routed"? Not very accurate, a common problem with markers of this sort, but at least it was placed near enough to the site of the confrontation. An older marker, a little farther along North Street, is more succinct: "In the revolution the first armed resistance to the Royal authority was made at this bridge 26 Feb. 1775 by the people of Salem. The advance of 300 British troops, led by Lt. Col. Leslie and sent by Gen. Gage to seize munitions of war, was here arrested." The phrase "armed resistance" is again misleading. On June 10th, the town of Salem dedicated Furlong Park on the north shore of the North River, one of whose four historical markers was devoted to "Salem in the American Revolution" and featured Leslie's retreat. The North River bridge itself does not cross the river; it is dammed at the foot of the overpass, and on the other side is a canal. The path of Leslie's retreat is now a tree-lined roadway: Lafayette Street in Salem to Pleasant Street and then Ocean Street in Marblehead. Small businesses, apartment blocks, and individual family homes line both sides of the broad road in Salem (after the fire in 1914 the road was widened); in Marblehead the streets are narrower and twisting. It ends at the Leslie's Cove condominiums, behind which a lovely garden affords a view of what had been called Homan's Cove. It is a not unpleasant two-and-a-half-hour walk (at a decent pace) from Derby Street in Salem. No marker reminds the traveler that Leslie and his men walked this route into history, however.

Those at the visitor's center and elsewhere at the Salem Maritime National Historic Site are knowledgeable about the raid, and a U.S. National Park Service montage on one of the pillars outside the visitor's center describes the event. Its account, however, is about as accurate as the markers. Despite what the montage's text says, the Intolerable Acts did not apply to the colonies as a whole, the Salem cannons were not removed to Concord, and the minutemen of Salem and the surrounding towns did not overawe the Regulars, much less impede their march into Salem. Nor did the minutemen raise the drawbridge.

The 64th Regiment of Foot is no longer a unit of the British Army, but it lives on in the form of uniformed reenactors in North Carolina, who "consistently strive to help to educate the public into the role of the British Soldier and the 64th Regiment of Foot during the period which we portray. We all love history, reenacting, our friendship with each other and this hobby. If you have the same spirit, the same goals, and are of a like mind, then we welcome you with open arms as a true comrade." After the evacuation of British troops from Boston, the 64th and Leslie served with distinction in Clinton's and Cornwallis's southern campaigns of 1780–1781.[19]

The research staff at the Peabody Essex Museum (PEM) has not forgotten the event. The museum's predecessor, the Essex Institute, had sponsored Charles M. Endicott's researches. The modern facility has been transformed from an elite organization where the town's leading men gathered into a public fixture open and inviting to all. The Peabody Museum and the Essex Institute own a number of historical buildings in and around Salem, and the museum itself is an architectural treasure. As the 2012 welcome by its director, Dan Monroe, explained: "There are many reasons to come to PEM. Sometimes, looking at a work of art with someone special by your side is all the motivation you need. Sitting in the light-filled Atrium, having lunch outside in the Garden Restaurant, watching the expression on a child's face as she makes a collage, each experience is worth the trip. PEM is the place to come for enjoyment, enrichment, sharing with family and friends, and creative stimulation." A small file on Leslie's retreat is preserved in the PEM's Phillips Library.[20]

Salem is today a tourist mecca, but not for its role in the coming of independence. Instead, Salem's tourism is tied to another event entirely: the witchcraft scare that resulted in over a hundred trials, nearly twenty executions, and the haunting cliché, "the Salem witch hunt." Historical markers and tourist sites for the witchcraft trials abound. On the streets one sees directions to the Witch Dungeon Museum, the Witch History Museum, the Witch House, the Witch Mansion, the Salem Witch Museum, and a wide variety of shops selling witchcraft trinkets, books, and tee shirts, and offering palm readings. The Salem Witch House (actually magistrate and merchant John Corwin's home), a New England saltbox-style dwelling, stands on the corner of North Street and Essex Street, not far from the spot where Barnard accosted Leslie.

When I spent a good deal of time in Salem twenty years ago researching the witchcraft trials, every bed-and-breakfast innkeeper, every museum docent, and everyone I talked to at the Peabody Essex Museum had an opinion on the witchcraft episode. The shelves at the museums and the local bookshops were lined with books on the witchcraft trials. Some of these mentioned the fact that one of the first magistrates to take testimony in Salem Village was John Hathorne, the ancestor of Nathaniel Hawthorne, the best-selling nineteenth-century short-story writer and novelist. Nathaniel Hawthorne worked at the customhouse on Derby Street, across from Richard Derby's long wharf; the latter was the spot where a column of Leslie's men swarmed during the raid. Farther down the street one finds the parking lot for the House of the Seven Gables, a mansion built in 1668 and the scene of one of Hawthorne's more popular novels, set in 1850. Its gothic aura (and Hawthorne's prose) recalled the witchcraft times, when "awe and terror brooded over the memories of those who died for this horrible crime of witchcraft."[21]

Why would such a horror story, a story that revealed the darker side of New England life, become so vital a part of Salem tourism, when Leslie's retreat, a tale of courage and honor, had all but vanished? One might cynically claim that Americans' fascination with the macabre outweighs their attachment to the heroic, but that simply is not true. For every one of the nearly one million people who visit Salem each year and pay admission to the Witch

House, there are two who visit the hallowed fields of Gettysburg. Can it be that patriotic gore is even more attractive to the American psyche than the incarceration, trial, and execution of the innocent for a crime they could not have committed? The founding members of the Essex Institute offer a clue.

On Friday, November 14, 1856, Samuel Fowler of Danvers presented a hour's worth of documentary evidence on the life and career of Samuel Parris. He blamed Parris, a foreigner (born in England, reared in Barbados) for the witchcraft crisis, though he believed that Parris was "honest" in his delusion about witches. The people of Salem were "courageous" in their decision to oppose Satan. Sitting in the audience, the Reverend Charles Upham added that people had made the mistake of putting too much faith in dreams. Bear in mind that Institute membership was determined through nominations by the founding members. It was, at first, a closed society, incorporated by the state of Massachusetts. Its purpose was not to find fault, but to give credit. When, in 1867, Salem's notables finally did confront the witchcraft outbreak in print, Charles Upham's two volumes on the witchcraft cases exonerated Salem, for it was "a delusion" that everyone shared. No one in authority was truly culpable, because everyone then believed in the existence of the Devil and the devilish power of witches. The "ideas and spirit" of the honest farmers of Salem Village were perverted by the unseemly quarrels that the Reverend Parris's incumbency stirred, and "the men and women of Salem were all victims of the superstition and fear of the times." Upham was "confident you will agree with me, that it was not because the people of Salem Village were more ignorant, stupid, or weak minded than people of other places," for "there was never a community composed originally of better materials, or better trained in all good uses." Like the men whose story Charles Moses Endicott told, the people of Salem Village "were energetic and intelligent," and their "moral condition, social intercourse, manners, and personal bearing were all excellent." One cannot miss how closely Fowler's and Upham's Salem Village inhabitants match Endicott's Salem townsmen—nothing had changed in the character of the people in the years between 1692 and 1775, and, by implication, between 1775 and the centennial in 1875.[22]

So long as Salem's history was in such hands, no critical study of witchcraft would be possible. That is now no longer the case. Salem does not control its own history and cannot spin that history to salve town pride. Despite the efforts of Salem's nineteenth-century historians, the witchcraft crisis attained status in national memory, while the gunpowder raid did not. Leslie's retreat remained a Salem story, never gaining the attention of mainstream accounts of the coming of the Revolution. By contrast, the trials of the witches became an American tragedy, firmly fixed in the psyche of the people, the pages of the textbooks, and the landscape of Salem itself, drawing visitors from all over the world.

There is, however, one final synergy: the Witch Trail Committee offers among its list of historic hiking trails the "Leslie's Retreat Trail," a ten-mile hike from Marblehead to Salem and back. "Allow 3 to 4 hours for the one way and 5 to 6 hours for the round trip." The trip includes the Marblehead town hall, the bridge over the South River (the Mill Pond Dam bridge), the site of the North Church, and the North River bridge. None of the originals of these sites remain, however, unlike those in Salem that belonged to the Corwin families. Entire blocks of the lovely Victorian mansions along Lafayette Street, built in the early nineteenth century with profits from the sea, vanished in the Great Fire of 1914. The hike does not include Leslie's Retreat Tavern or Leslie's Retreat Park, a favorite of local dog owners (websites warn visitors to watch their step), though they are close enough to the trail for a short excursion (a rest stop for thirsty tourists and their dogs, perhaps). Leslie's men had nothing to eat or drink except what they carried from the *Lively*. All of which leaves us with the question, why does Leslie's retreat still matter?[23]

𝕵𝕲 Epilogue

So much of the Salem gunpowder raid is frustrating, as there are more questions than answers. The easy questions concern the raid's immediate impact. The harder questions resist simple answers. Why did the raid—so important to contemporaries, invariably described in the first histories of the American Revolution—become an afterthought? Why did amateur local historians in the nineteenth century think the event was important, but professional historians in the twentieth century dismiss or ignore it? The answer seems to be that Lexington and Concord, Bunker Hill and the taking of Fort Ticonderoga, the siege of Boston and the invasion of Canada, all came to overshadow Leslie's retreat, because the key figures in those events would become the founding fathers of the nation, while happenstance left the protagonists at Salem behind. History loves the big battalions and the great men on horseback. One can accept or dismiss the views of local celebrants like Endicott, Loring, and Willson that the Salem gunpowder raid was the beginning of the Revolution, but serious study of the affair at Salem helps dispel some common misperceptions about the American Revolution and the Revolutionary War, interpretations that are driven by larger notions of how history happens.

The first of these lessons is that a military operation like the Salem raid, however meticulously it might have been planned, in real life plays out in a series of contingencies. Each decision that participants make, each action that they take, may—and often does—have unexpected consequences. Had Derby or Mason not given the order to raise the drawbridge leaf, the raid might have followed the course of the earlier incursion in Cambridge. Had someone fired a shot, a very different outcome might have ensued. Historical events great and small turn on such incidents. The insight at the core of this book is that the events at Salem—or, more precisely, the reports of the events at Salem—had a momentous influence on the conduct of the key players at Lexington and Concord. Then, too, contingency rather than the best-laid plans of both sides led to the first shots.

The next conclusion, a misperception, is that because it was so important, the Revolution should be seen as a whole, an ensemble production, in effect the big bang that birthed the American nation. This is an example of what philosopher Gilbert Ryle called the category mistake. In his telling, a university professor and a visitor were touring the campus. The professor showed the visitor the classrooms, the library, the laboratories, and the students. When the tour was done, the visitor was grateful but still wanted to know where the university was. The word had gained a concreteness apart from all the visible attributes that make up university life and work. Similarly, the American Revolution becomes a single, indivisible thing, an omnipresent whole moving through time, whereas Leslie's retreat teaches that the Revolution was a thousand little episodes, each distinct, each the product of individual and group choices.[1]

Third, the Salem raid suggests that one can dispense with the notion that the Revolutionary War was inevitable. It is an addiction for those who believe that great forces will always determine the outcome of events, and, like all addictions, this one cannot easily be broken. For the historian who sees events as the product of material forces, moral verities, or Providence, outcomes are always predetermined. The narrative historian may also see a kind of inevitability; the chief actors become "men [who] acquiesced in a growing sense that conflict was inevitable." Setting aside the philosophical question of historical inevitability, truly a mare's nest in any case, one can see from Salem's experience that later episodes of violence could have been averted. The outcome of the Salem gunpowder raid differed from the outcome of the Concord gunpowder raid precisely for the reasons Willson gave: "Had Colonel

Leslie been as rash at Salem as Major Pitcairn [or one of his subordinates] was at Lexington, in ordering his men to fire, what occurred in Middlesex [County] would in its main features have taken place in Essex [County]." Postponed, the violence might or might not have erupted.[2]

Fourth, the Salem episode hints that long-standing debates among historians about the origins of the Revolution may be overdrawn. The first of these debates concerns the leadership of the Revolution. Was it the plot of a cadre of leaders, or it was the work of the great mass of ordinary men? That debate ignores the lesson of Leslie's retreat. Leaders there were, and their impress on the Revolution was indelible. No one can discuss the larger story of the American Revolution without reference to a pantheon of greats, from John Adams to George Washington. But none of them were in Salem when Leslie arrived, unless one counts Timothy Pickering, and he was hardly the most visible man that day. Moreover, if the events of February 26th are any indication, the Revolution was not incited by insurgents seeking to emancipate the lower orders from the chains of upper-class oppression, nor was it begun by "the 'humble classes' who made the Revolution possible," the rank and file of the movement. It was Mason, Derby, Felt, and Barnard—middle-class men of property, hardly either the elite of the colony or its hewers of wood and drawers of water—who persuaded Leslie to retreat.[3]

But historians still are divided over how conservative or radical the Revolution was, a second debate that Leslie's retreat calls into question. Salem's conservative political leaders were loyalists like Lynde, Curwen, and Browne. Its patriot commanders were Derby, Pickering, and Felt. All were men of property and standing. While the sailors and dockworkers were ordinary men, there is no evidence that they were a coalition of radicals, "millennialist preachers, enslaved Africans, frontier mystics, and dockside tars." Conspirators like John Hancock and Samuel Adams—"every colony had a few radicals"—may have plotted mayhem, and a mob of apprentices, dockworkers, laborers, and shop boys may have pressed against the edges of the troops at Salem, but they did not determine the outcome of the raid.[4]

Fifth, and finally, although no one can doubt the intellectual achievements of the revolutionary leaders—as John Adams put it, the Revolution was a great time for an intellectual "to have been sent into life, at a time when the greatest law givers of antiquity would have wished to have [lived]"—the outcome of the gunpowder raid at Salem did not depend on new ideas of republican self-government, novel conceptions of rights, or invocations of ancient constitutions. The confrontation at the North River spawned exchanges of insults, not learned pamphlets. At Salem, simple things mattered, like a drawbridge leaf and bayonets. When revolutionary penmen came to rationalize the events, a military raid gained ideological meaning. But that was later.[5]

Leslie's retreat still matters, but not because it fits the current crop of historical theories and models. It matters because it mattered to contemporaries. The failed gunpowder raid empowered the minutemen. They mobilized and raced to Salem. It was a trial run for the confrontations at Lexington and Concord. It taught them—whether or not rightly—that faced with resolute armed men, the Regulars were not invincible, and amateur though the British might think them, colonial men-at-arms were not (as the Regulars told themselves) prone to run at the first shot.

Let us also not forget that the Salem gunpowder raid is a cracking good yarn, with genuine suspense, heroism, sacrifice, and a good ending, at least insofar as all concerned walked away unharmed that day. Every potentially deadly confrontation that ends with a negotiated settlement has a good ending—and provides a good lesson.

ACKNOWLEDGMENTS

My thanks to Irene Axelrod, Head Research Librarian at the Peabody Essex Museum (PEM) in Salem, for enthusiastic assistance and permission to reproduce the Perley/Phillips map and the Bridgman mural; to the research librarians at the William L. Clements Library, University of Michigan, for sharing a key piece of evidence from the Gage Papers archived there; to Betty Hunt, town historian of Marblehead, for information that led to Leslie's Cove; to Ryan Walsh, of the U.S. National Park Service, for his helpfulness during a research trip to Salem; to Michael Winship, N. E. H. Hull, and Williamjames Hoffer for comments on the project as it unfolded; and to Robert Brugger, Benjamin Carp, Robert Churchill, Donald Friary, Wayne E. Lee, and James Kirby Martin for reading a second draft of the manuscript and graciously suggesting improvements.

Donald Friary and I had what, for me, was a wonderful day in Salem and Marblehead. We looked for the Mill Pond Dam bridge site in Salem and Homan's Cove in Marblehead, no mean feat, given all that has changed in the two towns over the 240-plus years since the events narrated in the following pages. The two rivers that defined revolutionary-era Salem, the North and South Rivers, have been so shortened by road construction, landfill, channeling, and other "improvements," that the search for the landmarks of Leslie's route became a trip back in time.

Lynne Francis-Lunn, director of merchandising at the PEM, went beyond the call of duty to find the last copy of the 1937 Sidney Perley / James Duncan Phillips map of Salem in 1780. This map not only features the roads as they were then called, it indicates where householders lived. Using the map, it is possible to trace the Salem movements of the key figures in the raid.

Williamjames Hoffer and Louis Hoffer accompanied me on a final research trip to Salem, walking all over the terrain of the events, from the North River to Front Street in Marblehead. While we did not quite duplicate the route of the 64th Regiment of Foot, nor did we resemble Colonel Leslie and his fellow officers, we did share something of the wonder of imagining ourselves as part of an event that contributed to the American Revolution.

NOTES

PROLOGUE

1. Charles Moses Endicott, *An Account of Leslie's Retreat* (Salem, MA: Ives and Pease, 1856), 3; *Gentleman's Magazine*, April 17, 1775. Other occasions when colonists and Regulars faced off in gunpowder alarms and raids include Portsmouth, New Hampshire, on December 14, 1774, when a patriot mob attacked a small British garrison and seized powder and weapons. But none of these raids involved the British agreeing to retreat.

2. Weather information from *Salem Gazette*, February 28, 1775.

3. Actually, Leslie's rank at the time of the gunpowder raid was Lieutenant Colonel. He would, however, have been addressed as "Colonel," and I have followed that convention throughout.

CHAPTER ONE: The Most Loyal Town in the Province

1. In general, and the best, book on the Puritans' ideas and the planting of Massachusetts puritanism is Michael P. Winship, *Godly Republicanism: Puritans, Pilgrims, and a City on a Hill* (Cambridge, MA: Harvard University Press, 2012).

2. John Smith, *Description of New England* (London: Robert Clerke, 1616), 27.

3. Edmund S. Morgan, *Roger Williams: The Church and the State*, rev. ed. (New York: Norton, 2007), 27, 43, 44.

4. The best accounts of the growing inequality are Philip Greven, *Four Generations: Population, Land, and Family in Colonial Andover* (Ithaca, NY: Cornell University Press, 1972), 127–128; and Robert W. Gross, *The Minutemen and Their World* (New York: Hill and Wang, 1976), 194.

5. Narrative here and hereafter from Peter Charles Hoffer, *The Salem Witchcraft Trials: A Legal History* (Lawrence: University Press of Kansas, 1998), 35–53, 94–107; and Peter Charles Hoffer, *The Devil's Disciples: Makers of the Salem Witchcraft Trials* (Baltimore: Johns Hopkins University Press, 1996), 102–178.

6. James Duncan Phillips, *Salem in the Seventeenth Century* (Boston: Houghton Mifflin, 1933), 301. The fullest local account of the events, Charles Wentworth Upham's two-volume *Salem Witchcraft; With an Account of Salem Village* (Boston: Wiggin

and Lunt, 1867), devoted the second half of the first volume to demonstrating that everyone believed in witches and witchcraft then, and no one should condemn the people of Salem out of hand for the trials. Indeed, it was Salem's William Bradstreet, governor of the colony in 1680, who had bravely prevented an outbreak of witchcraft accusations at that time. "It is safe to say that, had he not been superceded by the arrival of Sir William Phipps as governor under the new charter, [the Salem witchcraft trials] would never have taken place" (1:451).

7. Architectural descriptions from Bryant Franklin Tolles Jr., Carolyn K. Tolles, and Paul F. Norton, *Architecture in Salem: An Illustrated Guide* (Salem, MA: Essex Institute, 1983), 127–128; and "Salem Architecture," Salem City Guide, www.salemweb .com/guide/arch/houses.shtml. On the favored-quarter theory in modern urban planning, Christopher B. Leinberger, *The Option of Urbanism: Investing in a New American Dream*, rev. ed. (Washington, DC: Island Press, 2008), 36; and Myron Orfield, *Metropolitics: A Regional Agenda for Community and Stability* (Washington, DC: Brookings Institute, 1997), 6.

8. Salem Maritime National Site visit, June 6, 2012.

9. Daniel Vickers and Vince Walsh, *Young Men and the Sea: Yankee Sailors in the Age of Sail* (New Haven, CT: Yale University Press, 2007), 204–209; Barry Levy, *Town Born: The Political Economy of New England from Its Founding to the Revolution* (Philadelphia: University of Pennsylvania Press, 2009), 87–88; and T. H. Breen, *The Marketplace of Revolution: How Consumer Politics Shaped American Independence* (New York: Oxford University Press, 2004), 53, 136.

10. Matthew G. Mackenzie, "Salem as Athenaeum," in Dane Anthony Morrison and Susan L. Schultz, eds., *Salem: Place, Myth, and Memory* (Lebanon, NH: University Press of New England, 2004), 98; Gardner, quoted in James Duncan Philips, *Salem in the Eighteenth Century* (Boston: Houghton Mifflin, 1937), 240. The description of the commercial elite appears in ibid., 241–252 and in U.S. National Park Service, *Salem: Maritime Salem in the Age of Sail*, National Park Handbook 126 (Salem, MA: Peabody Essex Museum, 2009), 24–25.

11. Lawrence B. Winer, "The Loyalists of Lynn, Salem, and Marblehead," master's thesis, Wayne State University (2008), 33; E. Alfred Jones, *The Loyalists of Massachusetts* (London: St. Catherine's, 1930); and Breen, *Marketplace*, 53.

12. Christopher White, "Salem as Religious Proving Ground," in Morrison and Schultz, *Salem*, 46–47.

13. Richard J. Morris, "Social Change, Republican Rhetoric, and the American Revolution: The Case of Salem, Massachusetts," *Journal of Social History* 31 (Winter 1997), 419–433.

14. T. A. Milford, *The Gardiners of Massachusetts: Provincial Ambition and the British-American Career* (Hanover, NH: University Press of New England, 2005), 109; Morris, "Social Change" 421; Winer, "Loyalists of Lynn," 45; and Sydney W. Jackman, "Letters of William Browne, American Loyalist," *Essex Institute Historical Collections* 96 (January 1960), 3–4. On deference and voting, Edward M. Cook, *The Fathers of the Towns: Leadership and Community Structure in Eighteenth-Century New England* (Baltimore:

Johns Hopkins University Press, 1976), 115–117, 192; and Richard Beeman, *The Varieties of Political Experience in Eighteenth-Century America* (Philadelphia: University of Pennsylvania Press, 2006), 92.

15. Instructions quoted in Phillips, *Salem in the Eighteenth Century*, 287; episode of the jackboot, ibid., 289; John Adams diary entry for January 10, 1766, quoted in *Works of John Adams*, ed. Charles Francis Adams (Boston, MA: Little, Brown, 1850), 2:176: "They were at first afraid of Salem, Newbury, Marblehead and Plymouth, but these Towns have agreed unanimously to the same Resolutions."

16. Phillips, *Salem in the Eighteenth Century*, 295.

17. Francis D. Cogliano, *Revolutionary America, 1763–1815: A Political History* (London: Taylor and Francis, 2008), 64; Pauline Maier, *From Resistance to Revolution: Colonial Radicals and the Development of American Opposition to Britain* (New York: Norton, 1991), 116; Breen, *Marketplace*, 227; and Salem Town Records, May 27, 1769, quoted in Phillips, *Salem in the Eighteenth Century*, 303.

18. Phillips, *Salem in the Eighteenth Century*, 306–307; John Adams, March 5, 1773, in Lyman Butterfield, ed., *Diary and Autobiography of John Adams* (Cambridge, MA: Harvard University Press, 1961), 2:79; and Hiller B. Zobel, *The Boston Massacre* (New York: Norton, 1996), 295.

19. Phillips, *Salem in the Eighteenth Century*, 309–311; Levy, *Town Born*, 184; and Gary Nash, *The Unknown American Revolution: The Unruly Birth of Democracy and the Struggle to Create America* (New York: Viking Penguin, 2006), 183.

20. Phillips, *Salem in the Eighteenth Century*, 317; T. H. Breen, *American Insurgents, American Patriots: The Revolution of the People* (New York: Hill and Wang, 2010), 93–99; and Nash, *Unknown American Revolution*, 58, 141.

21. Gordon S. Wood, *The Americanization of Benjamin Franklin* (New York: Penguin, 2005), 143.

22. In addition to the Port Act, the others were the Massachusetts Government Act (rescinding the charter of 1692), the Administration of Justice Act (removing trials of protestors to other colonies), and the repassage of the Quartering Act (housing British troops in public buildings). A lively summary of the newspapers' participation appears in Eric Burns, *Infamous Scribblers: The Founding Fathers and the Rowdy Beginnings of American Journalism* (New York: PublicAffairs Press, 2007), 163.

23. Peter Charles Hoffer, *Law and People in Colonial America*, 2nd ed. (Baltimore: Johns Hopkins University Press, 1998), 10–14, 141, 143.

24. Bernard Bailyn, *The Ordeal of Thomas Hutchinson* (Cambridge, MA: Harvard University Press, 1974), 214–215; Wood, *Americanization of Benjamin Franklin*, 144; Benjamin Woods Labaree, *The Boston Tea Party* (Boston: Northeastern University Press, 1979), 189–192; and Sidney George Fisher, *The Struggle for American Independence* (Philadelphia: Lippincott, 1908), 1:214.

25. John W. Shy, *Toward Lexington: The Role of the British Army in the Coming of the Revolution* (Princeton, NJ: Princeton University Press, 1965), 215; John C. Fredriksen, *Revolutionary War Almanac* (New York: Facts on File, 2006), 375; David Hackett Fischer, *Paul Revere's Ride* (New York: Oxford University Press, 1994), 34–35; Gage

to Lord Conway, March 25, 1766, in Clarence E. Carter, ed., *The Correspondence of General Thomas Gage* (New Haven, CT: Yale University Press, 1931), 1:85; and Gage's comments to the king, sent to Lord North by George III, quoted in "Report of the Council," *Proceedings of the American Antiquarian Society*, new ser., 1 (1882), 324.

26. Hoffer, *Law and People*, 2, 10–14, 141, 143; Alan Taylor, *The American Colonies* (New York: Viking, 2002), 286–288; and, on the origin of the governors-general, Charles McLean Andrews, *The Colonial Background of the American Revolution* (New Haven, CT: Yale University Press, 1924), 17.

27. See, e.g., Wayne Lee, *Barbarians and Brothers: Anglo-American Warfare, 1600–1815* (New York: Oxford University Press, 2011), 108.

28. "Address of the Justices of the Court to . . . Gage," May 24, 1774, in Peter Force, ed., *American Archives* (Washington, DC, 1837), 1:346. On Gage's arrival, Breen, *American Insurgents*, 71; and Fischer, *Paul Revere's Ride*, 41.

29. Gordon S. Wood, *The Radicalism of the American Revolution* (New York: Knopf, 1991), 38–39; "The Patriots of North America, a Sketch" [1775], quoted in Holly Brewer, *By Birth or Consent: Children, Law, and the Anglo-American Revolution in Authority* (Chapel Hill: University of North Carolina Press, 2005), 105.

30. Phillips, *Salem in the Eighteenth Century*, 262–263; Cogliano, *Revolutionary America*, 113. The list of signers: "John Sargent, Jacob Ashton, William Wetmore, James Grant, Henry Higginson, David Britton, P. G. Kast, Weld Gardner, Nathaniel Daubney, Richard Nicholls, William Cabot, Cabot Gerrish, William Gerrish, Rowland Savage, William Lilly, Jonathan Goodhue, John Prince, George Deblois, Andrew Dalgleish, Joseph Blaney, Archelaus Putnam, Samuel Porter, Thomas Poynton, Samuel Flagg, Nathan Goodale, William Pickman, C. Gayton Pickman, Nathaniel Sparhawk, William Vans, Timothy Orne, Richard Routh, Stephen Higginson, Benjamin Lynde, William Browne, John Turner, P. Frye, Francis Cabot, William Pynchon, John Fisher, John Mascarene, E. A. Holyoke, Jos. Bowditch, Ebenezer Putnam, S. Curwen, John Nutting, Jos. Dowse, Benjamin Pickman, and Henry Gardner."

31. These are collected in L. Kinvin Wroth, ed., *Province in Rebellion: A Documentary History of the Founding of the Commonwealth of Massachusetts, 1774–1775* (Cambridge, MA: Harvard University Press, 1975), quotation at 468.

32. Address to Governor Gage, June 21, 1774, quoted in Phillips, *Salem in the Eighteenth Century*, 325.

33. Susan Smith, "Biographical Sketch of Colonel David Mason of Salem, by His Daughter . . . June 1824," *Essex Institute Historical Collections* 48 (July 1912), 197–203.

34. Gerald Clarfield, *Timothy Pickering and the American Republic* (Pittsburgh: University of Pittsburgh Press, 1980), 3–11.

35. Clarfield, *Timothy Pickering*, 14–15.

36. James Duncan Phillips, *The Life and Times of Richard Derby, Merchant of Salem* (Cambridge, MA: Harvard University Press, 1929), 6 and after; and U.S. National Park Service, *Salem*, 29.

37. Charles M. Endicott, "Colonel Leslie's Retreat," *Proceedings of the Essex Institute* 1 (1856), 90; Richard Frothingham, *Life and Times of Joseph Warren* (Boston:

Little, Brown, 1856), 324; and John K. Alexander, *Samuel Adams: America's Revolutionary Politician* (Lanham, MD: Rowman and Littlefield, 2002), 134.

38. Timothy Pickering to Paine Wingate, August 25, 1774, quoted in Edward Hake Phillips, "Salem, Timothy Pickering, and the American Revolution," *Essex Institute Historical Collections* 111 (January 1975), 69; and Thomas Gage, proclamation, Salem, June 29, 1774, in Force, ed., *American Archives*, 1:491–492.

39. Phillips, *Salem in the Eighteenth Century*, 327–329; proclamation of Governor Gage, August 23, 1774, in Force, ed., *American Archives*, 1:729.

40. Edmund B. Willson, "Address," in City of Salem, *Memorial Exercises at the Centennial Anniversary of Leslie's Expedition to Salem . . . on Friday February 26, 1875* (Salem, MA, 1875), 78–81, seating diagram at 82. On the appearance of New England meetinghouses, Ola Elizabeth Winslow, *Meeting House Hill, 1630–1783* (New York: Macmillan, 1952), 53–54; Richard Rath, *How Early America Sounded* (Ithaca, NY: Cornell University Press, 2004), 107–108; and Peter Benes, *Meetinghouses of Early New England* (Amherst: University of Massachusetts Press, 2012), 15–16.

41. Proclamation by Governor Gage, September 28, 1774, in Force, ed., *American Archives*, 1:809; Endicott, "Colonel Leslie's Retreat," 95; and Jack Rakove, *Revolutionaries: A New History of the Invention of America* (New York: Houghton Mifflin Harcourt, 2010), 56–57.

42. Endicott, "Colonel Leslie's Retreat," 95; answer of Governor Gage to the Address of the Provincial Congress, October 17, 1774, in Force, ed., *American Archives*, 1:837.

43. John E. Ferling, *Almost A Miracle: The American Victory in the War for Independence* (New York: Oxford University Press, 2007), 66–67.

44. Lord Dartmouth to Thomas Gage, January 27, 1775, in Jared Sparks, ed., *The Writings of George Washington* (Boston: Little, Brown, 1855), 3:507.

CHAPTER TWO: Spies Like Us

1. Fred Anderson, *Crucible of War: The Seven Years' War and the Fate of Empire in British North America, 1754–1766* (New York: Knopf, 2000), 30–41. On the standing-army controversy, John Philip Reid, *In Defiance of the Law: The Standing-Army Controversy, the Two Constitutions, and the Coming of the American Revolution* (New York: New York University Press, 1981). Much of the general account of the wars in this chapter, and of the protests against Parliament that followed, is taken from Peter Charles Hoffer, *The History of the United States from the First Settlements to Reconstruction* (Indianapolis: College Network, 2001), ch. 5.

2. Ian K. Steele, *Warpaths: Invasions of North America* (New York: Oxford University Press, 1994), 175–183.

3. Anderson, *Crucible*, 24–25.

4. John Keegan, *Fields of Battle: The Wars for North America* (New York: Knopf, 1996), 121–133.

5. Douglas Edward Leach, "The British Army in America before 1775," in Jack P.

Greene and J. R. Pole, eds., *A Companion to the American Revolution* (New York: Wiley, 2000), 153; and Wolfe, quoted in Michael Stephenson, *Patriot Battles: How the War of Independence Was Fought* (New York: HarperCollins, 2008), 9.

6. Alan J. Guy, "The Army of the Georges, 1714–1783," in Ian Frederick William Beckett, ed., *Oxford History of the British Army* (Oxford: Oxford University Press, 2003), 97, 101; Tony Hayter, "The Army and the First British Empire, 1714–1783," in ibid., 118; Wayne E. Lee, *Barbarians and Brothers: Anglo-American Warfare, 1500–1865* (New York: Oxford University Press, 2011), 216; David Hackett Fischer, *Washington's Crossing* (New York: Oxford University Press, 2006), 33; Stephen Conway, *The British Isles and the American War for Independence* (New York: Oxford University Press, 1992), 14; and Hugh Percy, quoted in David Hackett Fischer, *Paul Revere's Ride* (New York: Oxford University Press, 1994), 254.

7. Walter R. Bourneman, *The French and Indian War* (New York: Harper, 2006), 273–279.

8. Allen Johnson, *A Prologue to Revolution: The Political Career of George Grenville* (Lanham, MD: University Press of America, 1997), 163–164, 174.

9. Richard White, *The Middle Ground: Indians, Empires, Republics in the Great Lakes Region, 1650–1815* (New York: Cambridge University Press, 1991), 287.

10. 5 Geo. III, chapter 33 (1765); Merrill Jensen, *The Founding of a Nation: The History of the American Revolution, 1763–1776* (New York: Oxford University Press, 1968), 213; and John Philip Reid, *The Constitutional History of the American Revolution: The Authority of Law* (Madison: University of Wisconsin Press, 2003), 22.

11. Adams, quoted in Ira Stoll, *Samuel Adams: A Life* (New York: Simon and Schuster, 2009), 62.

12. Charles Moses Endicott, *An Account of Leslie's Retreat* (Salem, MA: Ives and Pease, 1856), 12. The term "minutemen" was not official, but it existed for many years before the revolutionary crisis. In New England, it referred to those members of the militia who were assigned to respond immediately to the call to arms. It has gained notoriety in recent usage as a synonym for citizen groups patrolling the U.S.–Mexican border.

13. Norman K. Risjord, *The Revolutionary Generation* (Lanham, MD: Rowman and Littlefield, 2001), 45–46; John R. Galvin, *The Minute Men*, 2nd ed. (Washington, DC: Pergamon, 1989), 69–71; and Fischer, *Paul Revere's Ride*, 44–45.

14. Gage to Lord Dartmouth, February 17, 1775, in Jared Sparks, ed., *The Writings of George Washington* (Boston: Little, Brown, 1855); and Gage, instructions to Brown and DeBerniere, February 22, 1775, in Peter Force, ed., *American Archives* (Washington, DC, 1837), 1:1263.

15. Jerome Carter Hosmer, *The Narrative of General Gage's Spies* (Boston, 1912), has one, not entirely trustworthy version. The original was published by J. Gill, Boston, in 1779, from a manuscript allegedly left behind when the British forces left the city. Another version was reprinted in the *Massachusetts Historical Society Collections* for 1812. A third version was reprinted in Josiah H. Temple, *History of Framingham* (Framingham, 1887), 270–274. Hosmer reports that DeBerniere was an engineer and that the

sketches were his. Brown is identified in John Bakeless, *Turncoats, Traitors, and Heroes: Espionage in the American Revolution* (Philadelphia: Lippincott, 1959), 38. DeBerniere's sketch of the Bunker Hill battle survives in "Maps of the Revolutionary Period," in Justin Windsor, ed., *Memorial History of Boston* (Boston: Osgood, 1882), 3:xvi.

16. Adrien Jacquinot, "An Historical Sketch of Harvard University," in Moses King, ed., *The Harvard Register: An Illustrated Monthly* (Cambridge, MA: published at Harvard College, 1881), 3:388.

17. Robert W. Gross, *The Minutemen and Their World*, rev. ed. (New York: Hill and Wang, 2001), 79–80; Bernard Bailyn, *Voyagers to the West* (New York: Knopf, 1986), 3–4; and Fischer, *Paul Revere's Ride*, 97. On Ploughjogger, a comic figure that John Adams invented in 1767, Helen S. Saltman, "John Adams' Earliest Essays: The Humphrey Ploughjogger Letters," *William and Mary Quarterly*, 3rd ser., 37 (January 1980), 125–135.

18. Alan Taylor, *The American Colonies* (New York: Viking, 2002), 443.

19. Smith, quoted in Ruma Chopra, *Unnatural Rebellion: Loyalists in New York City during the Revolution* (Charlottesville: University of Virginia Press, 2011), 3; and Joseph Galloway, *The Claim of the American Loyalists Viewed and Maintained* (London: Wilkie, [1781] 1788), 5. On Johnson's efforts, Elizabeth P. McCaughey, *From Loyalist to Founding Father: The Political Odyssey of William Samuel Johnson* (New York: Columbia University Press, 1980), 168–175. On Galloway's efforts, John E. Ferling, *The Loyalist Mind: Joseph Galloway and the American Revolution* (State College: Pennsylvania State University Press, 1991), 112–127.

20. John Noble Wilford, *The Mapmakers* (New York: Random House, 2001), 206; and John Ferling, *The Ascent of George Washington* (New York: Bloomsbury Press, 2010), 12–13.

21. On slavery in Massachusetts and the petitions for freedom, B. Eugene McCarthy and Thomas L. Doughton, eds., *From Bondage to Belonging: The Worcester Slave Narratives* (Amherst: University of Massachusetts Press, 2007), xxviii, xxx. On watch and warn, Peter Charles Hoffer, "Courts and Law in British North America," in Kermit Hall, ed., *Oxford Companion to American Law* (New York: Oxford University Press, 2002), 367.

22. T. H. Breen, *American Insurgents, American Patriots: The Revolution of the People* (New York: Hill and Wang, 2010), 46; and Gordon S. Wood, *The Radicalism of the American Revolution* (New York: Knopf, 1992), 145.

23. Alexander Hamilton, "Itinerarium," in Wendy Martin, ed., *Colonial American Travel Narratives* (New York: Penguin, 1994), 178, 179, 181, 184, 182, 186, 197.

24. Peter Thompson, *Rum Punch and Revolution: Taverngoing and Public Life in Eighteenth-Century Philadelphia* (Philadelphia: University of Pennsylvania Press, 1999), 154; Silas Deane to Elizabeth Deane, September 5, 1774, in Paul H. Smith et al., eds., *Letters of Delegates to Congress, 1774–1789* (Washington, DC: Library of Congress, 1976–), 1:15; and David W. Conroy, *In Public Houses: Drink and the Revolution of Authority in Colonial Massachusetts* (Chapel Hill: University of North Carolina Press, 1995), 257–258, 262–263.

25. William D. Brewer, "Race and Miscegenation on Stage," in Frederick Burwick, Nancy Moore Goslee, and Diane Long Hoeveler, eds., *Encyclopedia of Romantic Literature* (Hoboken, NJ: Wiley-Blackwell, 2012), 1083.

26. Ian Janssen, "Maps and Cartography," in Stanley Sandler, ed., *Ground Warfare: An International Encyclopedia* (Santa Barbara, CA: ABC-CLIO, 2002), 1:538; and Yolande Hodson, "Military Surveys, 1700–1900," in Helen Wallis and Anita McConnell, eds., *Historians' Guide to Early British Maps* (Cambridge: Cambridge University Press, 1995), 27–28.

27. George Lee Haskins, *Law and Authority in Early Massachusetts* (New York: Macmillan, 1960), 88; and Daniel Dorcester, *Christianity in the United States from the First Settlement Down To the Present Time* (New York: Hunt and Eaton, 1895), 217.

28. Edward Field, *The Colonial Tavern* (Providence, RI: Preston, 1897), 40–41; and Conroy, *In Public Houses*, 235–236.

29. Ray Raphael, "Blacksmith Timothy Bigelow and the Massachusetts Revolution of 1774," in Alfred F. Young, Gary B. Nash, and Ray Raphael, eds., *Revolutionary Founders: Rebels, Radicals, and Reformers in the Making of the Nation* (New York: Knopf, 2011), 35–52.

30. Richard J. Hooker, *A History of Food and Drink in America* (Indianapolis: Bobbs, Merrill, 1981), 81; and Andrew F. Smith, ed., *Oxford Companion to Food and Drink* (New York: Oxford University Press, 2007), 68.

31. Clifford K. Shipton, *New England Life in the Eighteenth Century* (Cambridge, MA: Harvard University Press, 1995), 10.

32. Meeting of the Committee of Safety, March 14, 1775, in Benjamin Lincoln, ed., *The Journals of Each Provincial Congress of Massachusetts in 1774 and 1775, and the Committee of Safety* (Boston: Dutton, 1838), 513. On the warning-out system, which was not abolished until 1793, Josiah Henry Benton, *Warning Out in New England* (Boston: Clarke, 1911), 114.

33. Fischer, *Paul Revere's Ride*, 263. Bigelow rose from captain to major to colonel in the months between the summer of 1774 and the Battle of Bunker Hill, Worcester having chosen him to attend the provincial congress in Cambridge as well. E. B. Crane, "Early Paper Mills in Massachusetts," *Proceedings of the Worcester Society of Antiquity* (Worcester, MA: The Society, 1888), 7:119–120. "Rough music" might include riding someone out of town on a rail, tarring and feathering, tearing down houses, and the like, as well as, on occasion, attacking troops with stones and ice balls. But no one shot at the guards during the Boston Massacre. Paul Gilje, *Rioting in America* (Bloomington: Indiana University Press, 1996), 47. On the Committees of Safety, Agnes Hunt, *The Provincial Committees of Safety of the American Revolution* (Boston: Winn and Judson, 1904), 12–14; and Harry A. Cushing, *History of the Transition from Provincial to Commonwealth Governments in Massachusetts* (New York: Columbia University Press, 1896), 140.

34. Timothy Pickering Jr., *An Easy Plan of Discipline for a Militia* (Salem, MA: Hall, 1775), 5; Gerald Clarfield, *Timothy Pickering and the American Republic* (Pittsburgh: University of Pittsburgh Press, 1980), 31; Sharon V. Salinger, *Taverns and Drinking*

in Early America (Baltimore: Johns Hopkins University Press, 2004), 154; and John Martin Carroll and Colin F. Baxter, *The American Military Tradition* (Lanham, MD: Rowman and Littlefield, 2007), 5. Michael Bellesiles (*Arming America* [New York: Soft Skull Press, 2003], 170, 173) finds that the colonial militia on the eve of the Revolutionary War was poorly armed, worse trained, and did not perform well. Differing opinions appear in Robert H. Churchill, "Gun Ownership in Early America: A Survey of Manuscript Militia Returns," *William and Mary Quarterly*, 3rd ser., 60 (July 2003), 625–627; and Ronald L. Boucher, "The Colonial Militia as a Social Institution: Salem, Massachusetts, 1764–1775," *Military Affairs* 37 (December 1973), 126. For the militia count, Clarfield, *Timothy Pickering*, 30.

35. Sidney Perley, *Historic Storms of New England* (Salem, MA: Salem Press, 1891), 129.

36. John Henry Stark, *Loyalists of Massachusetts* (Boston: J. H. Stark, 1907), 400.

37. Collection guide, Israel Williams papers, Massachusetts Historical Society.

38. Fischer, *Paul Revere's Ride*, 67.

39. Sarah Kemble Knight, *The Journal of Madam Knight* (Bedford, MA, [1704] 1825), 11. The journal was not the work of Knight, nor did it originate in 1704. The depiction, however, is accurate enough. Alan Margolies, "The Editing and Publication of the *Journal of Madam Knight*," *Papers of the Bibliographical Society of America* 58 (March 1964), 25–32.

40. Memoranda from the Gage Papers, Clements Library, University of Michigan, reproduced in James Duncan Phillips, "Why Colonel Leslie Came to Salem," *Essex Institute Historical Collections* 90 (October 1954), 314; Ellen Chase, *The Beginnings of the American Revolution* (New York: Baker and Taylor, 1910), 2:242; and Gross, *Minutemen and Their World*, 112.

CHAPTER THREE: Leslie's Retreat

1. Charles M. Endicott, "The Endicott Family of Salem," *New England Historical and Genealogical Register* 1 (1847), 335–342; Robert Booth, *Death of an Empire: The Rise and Murderous Fall of Salem, America's Richest City* (New York: St. Martin's, 2011), 245–252; and Vanita Shastri, *The Salem India Story* (Lexington, MA: Meru, 2008), 17.

2. *Essex Institute Historical Collections* 1 (1859), 1.

3. Endicott's account appeared in two places: a short book (Charles Moses Endicott, *An Account of Leslie's Retreat* [Salem, MA: Ives and Pease, 1856]) and in Charles M. Endicott, "Colonel Leslie's Retreat," *Proceedings of the Essex Institute* 1 (1856). In the latter, it began on page 90; the page for the separately printed account is page 1. On the great hall and the building, U.S. National Park Service, *Salem: Maritime Salem in the Age of Sail*, National Park Handbook 126 (Salem, MA: Peabody Essex Museum, 2009), 151; and Bryant F. Tolles Jr., *Architecture in Salem* (Hanover, NH: University Press of New England, 1983), 4–5. Note that the present building in the Phillips Library complex next to Plummer Hall, with Essex Institute carved on its lintel, was not used by the Institute until 1883.

4. John Brewer, *The Sinews of Power: War, Money, and the English State, 1688–1873* (New York: Knopf, 1990), 39–40; Harlow Giles Unger, *John Hancock: Merchant King and American Patriot* (Hoboken, NJ: Wiley, 2000), 188–189; and Ellen Chase, *The Beginnings of the American Revolution* (New York: Baker and Taylor, 1910), 2:241.

5. Chase, *American Revolution*, 2:241.

6. Larry H. Addington, *Patterns of War since the Eighteenth Century* (Bloomington: Indiana University Press, 1994), 12–13; Jonathan B. A. Bailey, *Field Artillery and Fire Power* (Annapolis, MD: Naval Institute Press, 1994), 172; and John W. Shy, *A People Numerous and Armed: Reflections on the Military Struggle for American Independence*, rev. ed. (Ann Arbor: University of Michigan Press, 1990), 85, 87.

7. John R. Alden, *General Gage in America* (Baton Rouge: Louisiana State University Press, 1948), 181; and "The Affair at the North Bridge, Salem, February 26, 1775," *Essex Institute Historical Collections* 38 (1902), 325–327.

8. Gage to Leslie, January 14, 1775, Gage Papers, Clements Library, University of Michigan. I am grateful to militia expert Robert Churchill for his information on "a stand of arms."

9. David Hackett Fischer, *Paul Revere's Ride* (New York: Oxford University Press, 1994), 374. Still, the urge to recreate a conversation between Gage and Leslie was almost too tempting to forgo.

10. Thomas Gage to Lt. Colonel Leslie, January 14, 1775, Gage Papers, Clements Library, University of Michigan; and Endicott, *An Account*, 39.

11. Endicott, *An Account*, 2; John Wesley Hanson, *History of the Town of Danvers* (Danvers, MA, 1848), 1:82; Elbridge Henry Goss, *The Life of Paul Revere* (Boston: Cupples, 1891), 1:175; "HMS *Lively* (1756)," http://en.wikipedia.org/wiki/HMS_Lively_(1756)/; and "Post ship," http://en.wikipedia.org/wiki/Post_ship/.

12. Neil R. Stout, *The Royal Navy in America* (Annapolis, MD: Naval Institute Press, 1973), 96; David Hackett Fischer, *Washington's Crossing* (New York: Oxford University Press, 2006), 66–68; and Ira D. Gruber, *The Howe Brothers and the American Revolution* (Chapel Hill: University of North Carolina Press, 2011), 49.

13. "A detachment" of 400 is in Thomas Gage to Lord Dartmouth, March 4, 1775, in Jared Sparks mss., Harvard College Library, reprinted in Robert S. Rantoul, ed., *A Collection of Historical and Biographical Pamphlets* (Salem, MA: Essex Institute, 1881), 24; the 140 figure is from Abiel Holmes, *American Annals* (Cambridge, MA: Hilliard, 1805), 2:203; the 240 figure is from William Gordon, *The History of the Rise, Progress, and Establishment of the Independence of the United States of America* (London: Dilly and Buckland, 1788), 1:470; "a small detachment" is in Charles Stedman, *The History of the Origin, Progress, and Termination of the American War* (Dublin, 1794), 1:113; and the muster count appears in Fischer, *Paul Revere's Ride*, 309 (appendix F). In the fall of 1963, at the University of Rochester, Willson Havelock Coates explained to his undergraduate honors seminar why the lower count was best. I have never forgotten—or, to my disappointment, duplicated—the lucidity of his presentation.

14. Maurice Matloff, *American Military History, 1775–1902* (New York: Da Capo, [1969] 1996), 1:21; Jeremy Black, *European Warfare in a Global Context, 1660–1815*

(London: Taylor and Francis, 2007), 32–33; and Matthew H. Spring, *With Zeal and Bayonets Only: The British Army on Campaign in North America, 1775–1783* (Norman: University of Oklahoma Press, 2008), 121.

15. Rudyard Kipling, "Brown Bess," in *The Works of Rudyard Kipling* (New York: Doubleday, 1911), 1:61; and Richard Holmes, *Redcoat: The British Soldier in the Age of Horse and Musket* (New York: Norton, 2001), 194–195.

16. "HMS Lively," http://en.wikipedia.org/wiki/HMS_Lively_(1756)/.

17. John Bailey of Rowley, Massachusetts, describing a trip on the twenty-gun port ship HMS *Hind* from Boston to London in 1760, quoted in John Robinson and George Francis Dow, *The Sailing Ships of New England, 1607–1907* (Salem, MA: Marine Research Society, 1928), 39; and Fischer, *Paul Revere's Ride*, 58. The search for the landing spot took a day in Marblehead; the good offices of the city's historian, Betty Hunt; and, above all, the good humor, knowledge, and patience of my guide, Donald Friary. Once named Homan's Cove, then Atkins Beach, today the cove is called Leslie's Cove, named after Colonel Leslie. "Was not a happy one" is, I hope, a most ingenious paraphrase of the "Policeman's Song" in Gilbert and Sullivan's comic opera, *The Pirates of Penzance*. Weather system information comes from the author's six years in Cambridge, traveling often to Worcester and Salem in winter.

18. A collection of these is in Simon Dickie, *Cruelty and Laughter: Forgotten Comic Literature and the Unsentimental Eighteenth Century* (Chicago: University of Chicago Press, 2011), 122 and after.

19. Endicott, *An Account*, 1; Samuel Roads, *History and Traditions of Marblehead* (Marblehead, MA, 1881), 111; and Fischer, *Paul Revere's Ride*, 59–62.

20. Endicott, *An Account*, 15.

21. Endicott, *An Account*, 20; Hanson, *History of the Town*, 82; Chase, *American Revolution*, 2:251.

22. Brian Donahue, *The Great Meadow: Farmers and the Land in Colonial Concord* (New Haven, CT: Yale University Press, 2007), 92; William Cronon, *Changes in the Land: Indians, Colonists, and the Ecology of New England*, rev. ed. (New York: Hill and Wang, 2003), 128; and Alexander Garden, *Anecdotes of the Revolutionary War in America* (Charleston[, SC]: Miller, 1822), 124. The British spiked cannons when they could not be moved. Hannah Winthrop to Mercy Warren, September 27, 1774, "Warren–Adams Letters," *Massachusetts Historical Society Proceedings* (Boston: Massachusetts Historical Society, 1912), 72:32, n2.

23. This and the following anecdotes, where not otherwise credited, appear in Endicott, *An Account*, 21–47. For this paragraph, see also George B. Loring, "Address," in City of Salem, *Memorial Exercises at the Centennial Anniversary of Leslie's Expedition to Salem . . . on Friday February 26, 1875* (Salem, MA, 1875), 47.

24. James Duncan Phillips, *Salem in the Seventeenth Century* (Boston: Houghton Mifflin, 1933), 344–345. Street names and directions from "Map of Salem, about 1780, based on the researches of Samuel Perley, drawn by Henry Noyes Otis," James Duncan Phillips, copyright 1937, courtesy of the Peabody Essex Museum (PEM), used by permission.

25. Chase, *American Revolution*, 2:252

26. Distance across the river at the bridge site from the Sidney Perley / James Duncan Phillips "Map of Salem," courtesy of the PEM, used by permission. Personal observation confirmed the distance, although both shorelines have changed greatly since 1775.

27. On personality differences, Steven L. Allen, Peter C. Hoffer, and N. E. H. Hull, "Choosing Sides: A Quantitative Study of the Psychological Determinants of Political Affiliation," *Journal of American History* 65 (1978), 344–366.

28. Loring, "Address," 48–49.

29. Susanne Saville, *Hidden Salem* (Salem, MA: History Press, 2010), 63.

30. "Teague" suggests that the catcaller was an Irishman, but he might have been anyone, for the name Teague came to be associated with rough and cunning rascals in American popular literature in the early nineteenth century. See, e.g., Hugh Henry Brackenridge, *Modern Chivalry: Containing the Adventures of a Captain and Teague O'Regan, His Servant*, 4 vols. (Richmond, VA, 1792–1797). As one modern editor of Brackenridge explains, "the servant is never described because 'the very name imports what he was'" (Daniel Marder, ed., *A Hugh Henry Brackenridge Reader* [Pittsburgh: University of Pittsburgh Press, 1970], 32). Thus the anecdote might have been invented long after the event, and the speaker given the name to suggest the character of the men sitting on the far side of the bridge and the kind of insults they were shouting, rather than any particular man and any particular insult.

31. Fischer, *Paul Revere's Ride*, 78 (plans), 85 (orders not to kill or destroy).

32. Daniel Vickers, *Farmers and Fishermen; Two Centuries of Work in Essex County, Massachusetts, 1630–1830* (Chapel Hill: University of North Carolina Press, 1994), 140; Barry Levy, *Town Born: The Political Economy of New England from Its Founding to the Revolution* (Philadelphia: University of Pennsylvania Press, 2009), 170, 172; and Hiller B. Zobel, *The Boston Massacre* (New York: Norton, 1996), 182.

33. Marcus Rediker, *The Slave Ship: A Human History* (New York: Viking, 2007), 203; and Roald Kverndal, *Seaman's Missions: Their Origins and Early Growth* (Elizabethton, TN: William Carey Library, 1986), 242.

34. Endicott, *An Account*, 30.

35. Retreat was and remains the subject of military science. See, e.g., Carl Von Clausewitz, "Retreat after a Lost Battle," in *On War*, trans. J. J. Graham (Lawrence, KS: Digirreads, [1827] 2008), 176. For more recent investigations, Eric Hammel, *Chosin: Heroic Ordeal of the Korean War* (Pacifica, CA: Pacifica, 1981), 31. On Smith, Clifton La Bree, *The Gentle Warrior: General Oliver Prince Smith, USMC* (Kent, OH: Kent State University Press, 2001), 8.

36. Endicott, *An Account*, 32, quoting the account of John Howard, a Marblehead militiaman who was at the scene.

37. Octavius Pickering, *The Life Of Timothy Pickering* (Boston: Little, Brown, 1867), 1:60–63. Pickering and his gallant forty had made their way back to the bridge in the popular imagination. See, e.g., *Salem Post*, March 3, 1875; William B. Dennis, "North Salem," *[Salem] Saturday Evening Observer*, June 29, 1912, 1.

38. Endicott, *An Account*, 41,

39. Endicott, *An Account*, 43.

40. Abstract of a manuscript, "Memoir of My Father Colonel David Mason, Written by his Daughter," quoted in Endicott, *An Account*, 45.

41. Ralph Delahaye Paine, *The Ships and Sailors of Old Salem* (Chicago: McClurg, 1912), 155.

42. Endicott, *An Account*, 47. On Church, Thomas B. Allen, *Tories: Fighting for the King in American's First Civil War* (New York: HarperCollins, 2011), 43–44.

43. "In pamphlet after pamphlet the American writers cited Locke on natural rights" (Bernard Bailyn, *The Ideological Origins of the American Revolution*, rev. ed. [Cambridge, MA: Harvard University Press, 1992], 27); and John Locke, *Two Treatises of Government*, ed. Peter Laslett (Cambridge: Cambridge University Press, [1690] 1967), 304.

44. Thomas Jefferson, "A Summary View of the Rights of British America" [1774], in Paul L. Ford, ed., *The Works of Thomas Jefferson* (Washington, DC: G. P. Putnam's Sons, 1904), 2:65; and Richard L. Bushman, *King and People* (Chapel Hill: University of North Carolina Press, 1986), 204.

45. Endicott, *An Account*, 40; and James Barr Curwen, "Reminiscences of Capt. James Barr of Salem, Mass.," *Essex Institute Historical Collections* 27 (1890), 123–148.

CHAPTER FOUR: Intended and Unintended Consequences

1. Elbridge Henry Goss, *The Life of Paul Revere* (Boston: Cupples, 1891), 1:174–175; Ezra Stiles, *Diary of Ezra Stiles* (New York: C. Scribner, 1901), 1:522, 523; and Gerald Clarfield, *Timothy Pickering and the American Republic* (Pittsburgh: University of Pittsburgh Press, 1980), 30.

2. Isaiah Thomas, *The History of Printing in America* (Philadelphia: Munsell, 1874), 1:177–178; and James Duncan Phillips, *Salem in the Seventeenth Century* (Boston: Houghton Mifflin, 1933), 346.

3. *Essex Gazette*, February 28, 1775.

4. *Massachusetts Spy*, March 2, 1775.

5. [Timothy Pickering,] "Letter to the Editor," *Essex Gazette*, March 7, 1775; and Octavius Pickering, *The Life Of Timothy Pickering* (Boston: Little, Brown, 1867), 1:62.

6. Cited in Robert W. Gross, *The Minutemen and Their World*, rev. ed. (New York: Hill and Wang, 2001), 112.

7. Thomas, *History of Printing in America*, 387–388; and *(Boston) Massachusetts Gazette*, March 1, 1775.

8. Thomas Gage to Lord Dartmouth, March 4, 1775, in Jared Sparks mss., Harvard College Library, reprinted in Robert S. Rantoul, "Some Claims of Salem on the Notice of the Country" [1894], *Essex Institute Historical Collections* 32 (1896), 24.

9. *Lloyd's Evening Post and British Chronicle*, May 29–31, 1775; and Edmund Burke, quoted in Rantoul, "Some Claims of Salem," 14.

10. John W. Shy, *A People Numerous and Armed: Reflections on the Military Struggle*

for American Independence, rev. ed. (Ann Arbor: University of Michigan Press, 1990), 89, 104; Harlow Giles Unger, *John Hancock: Merchant King and American Patriot* (Hoboken, NJ: Wiley, 2000), 191; and David Hackett Fischer, *Paul Revere's Ride* (New York: Oxford University Press, 1994), 86–87.

11. D. Michael Ryan, *Concord and the Dawn of Revolution* (Charleston, SC: History Press, 2007), 52–53; and Fischer, *Paul Revere's Ride*, 96–112, 313–314 (appendix K). John Howe's account, *The Journal Kept by Mr. John Howe, while He Was in Service as a British Spy*, appeared in print in Concord, New Hampshire, in 1827, just in time for the fiftieth anniversary of independence. This work, with a few changes, was from Luther Roby's copy of DeBerniere's journal, as noted in Daniel E. Williams, "Specious Spy: The Narrative Lives—and Lies—of Mr. John Howe," *Eighteenth Century: Theory and Interpretation* 34 (1993), 264–286. Esther Forbes (*Paul Revere and the World He Lived In* [Boston: Houghton, 1948], 243–248) bought the story of John Howe the spy hook, line, and sinker, not recognizing the plagiarism from DeBerniere's journal.

12. This account relies on Fischer, *Paul Revere's Ride*, 149–150, 188–199.

13. Fischer, *Paul Revere's Ride*, 193–194.

14. Fischer, *Paul Revere's Ride*, 148. Fischer, usually so clear, in this instance is impenetrable. On contingency, Eugene Genovese, *From Rebellion to Revolution: Afro-American Slave Revolts in the Making of the Modern World* (Baton Rouge: Louisiana State University Press, 1979), 3; and Malcolm Gladwell, *The Tipping Point: How Little Things Can Make a Big Difference* (Boston: Little, Brown, 2000), introduction.

15. Evelyn and Pitcairn, quoted in Stephen Conway, *The War of American Independence, 1775–1783* (London: Edward Arnold, 1995), 19–20. Pitcairn was writing two weeks before the Salem gunpowder raid, but news of it could not have changed his attitude. "Damn you" is quoted in Fischer, *Paul Revere's Ride*, 191.

16. Fischer, *Paul Revere's Ride*, 208–212, 320–321.

17. Robert Crowley, *What If?* (New York: Berkley, 2004), xii.

18. In his classic study of the Boston Tea Party, Benjamin Woods Labaree concluded that the violence attending the tossing of tea into Boston Harbor, followed by the parliamentary Port Act, meant that the American Revolution could only be achieved through war; a peaceable transition was impossible after the tea party (*Boston Tea Party*, 264). I respectfully disagree, as I think Leslie's retreat demonstrated.

19. Clarfield, *Timothy Pickering*, 31.

20. Eliga Gould, *The Persistence of Empire; British Political Culture in the Age of the American Revolution* (Chapel Hill: University of North Carolina Press, 2000), 190–191; and Fischer, *Paul Revere's Ride*; 275–279.

21. Robert S. Rantoul, "Voyage of the *Quero*," *Essex Institute Historical Collections* 36 (1902), 1–30; Fischer, *Paul Revere's Ride*, 279–280; and Charles Royster, *A Revolutionary People at War: The Continental Army and American Character, 1775–1783* (Chapel Hill: University of North Carolina Press, 1980), 11–12.

22. James L. Nelson, *With Fire and Sword: The Battle of Bunker's Hill and the Beginning of the American Revolution* (New York: Macmillan, 2011), 235 and after (on Clinton's and Howe's roles), 302 (on the death of Warren); and Gage to Lord

Barrington, June 26, 1775, quoted in Thomas J. Fleming, *The Story of Bunker Hill* (New York: Collier, 1962), 316.

23. John R. Alden, *A History of the American Revolution* (New York: Knopf, 1969), 166–167; Peter Oliver, *Origin and Progress of the American Rebellion*, ed. Douglas Adair and John A. Schutz (Stanford, CA: Stanford University Press, [1781] 1961), 121; and John Trumbull, *Tom Gage's Proclamation Versified* (New York, 1775), 1.

24. [John Trumbull,] "McFingal: A Modern Epic Poem," Canto II, *Connecticut Courant*, August 14, 1775. On the "Fingal" and Macpherson controversy, Dafydd Moore, "The Reception of *The Poems of Ossian* in England and Scotland," in Howard Gaskill, ed., *The Reception of* Ossian *in Europe* (London: Continuum, 2004) 30–31, 39–40.

25. Phillips, *Salem in the Eighteenth Century*, 369–373; James Barr Curwen, "Reminiscences of Capt. James Barr of Salem, Mass.," *Essex Institute Historical Collections* 27 (1890), 123–148; and U.S. National Park Service, *Salem: Maritime Salem in the Age of Sail*, National Park Handbook 126 (Salem, MA: Peabody Essex Museum, 2009), 38–39.

26. "Address to the Committee of Safety of Salem, May 30, 1775," *Essex Gazette*, June 1, 1775.

27. "A Worcester Farmer," *Gage's Folly, or the Tall Fox Outwitted* (Salem, MA: E. Russell, 1776), 1; and Joseph Galloway, *The Claim of the American Loyalists Viewed and Maintained* (London: Wilkie, [1781] 1788), vii.

28. Phillips, *Salem in the Eighteenth Century*, 381–387; and Sarah Purcell, *Sealed with Blood: War, Sacrifice, and Memory in Revolutionary America* (Philadelphia: University of Pennsylvania Press, 2002), 68.

29. John R. Alden, *General Gage in America* (Baton Rouge: Louisiana State University Press, 1948), 291.

30. Hugh Thomas, *The Slave Trade: The Story of the Atlantic Slave Trade, 1440–1870* (New York: Simon and Schuster, 2007), 350; James A. Rawley, *The Transatlantic Slave Trade: A History* (New York: Norton, 1981), 302; and *Correspondence on Slave Trade with Foreign Powers: Sessional Papers of the House of Lords, 1842* (London: Her Majesty's Government, 1842), 13:218.

31. Edward Gray, *William Gray, of Salem, Merchant* (Boston: Houghton Mifflin, 1914), 41; Charles Stuart Osgood and Henry Morrill Batchelder, *Historical Sketch of Salem, 1626–1879* (Salem, MA: Essex Historical Institute, 1879), 220–221; Michael Connolly and Mary Beth Connolly, "New England Industry and Workers," in Mark R. Cheathem, ed., *Jacksonian and Antebellum Age: People and Perspectives* (Santa Barbara, CA: ABC-CLIO, 2008), 118–119; and Barbara M. Tucker and Kenneth H. Tucker, *Industrializing Antebellum America* (New York: Macmillan, 2008), 172.

CHAPTER FIVE: Memorial Exercises

1. Alfred Young, *The Shoemaker and the Tea Party* (Boston: Beacon, 1999), 186.

2. Gordon Wood, *The Radicalism of the American Revolution* (New York: Knopf,

1991), 300–301 and after; Gordon Wood, *Empire of Liberty: A History of the Early Republic* (New York: Oxford University Press, 2009), 253 and after; and Alan Taylor, *William Cooper's Town: Power and Persuasion on the Frontier of the Early American Republic* (New York: Knopf, 1995), 157 and after.

3. Joseph A. Conforti, *Imagining New England: Explorations of Regional Identity from the Pilgrims to the Mid-Twentieth Century* (Chapel Hill: University of North Carolina Press, 2000), 204.

4. Eric Foner, *Reconstruction: America's Unfinished Revolution, 1863–1877* (New York: Harper, 1988), 569; Paul Buck, *Road to Reunion, 1865–1900* (New York: Random House, 1937); and the editor of *Scribner's Magazine*, quoted in Buck, *Road to Reunion*, at 134.

5. J. S. Ingram, *Centennial Exposition Described and Illustrated* (Philadelphia: Hubbard, 1876), 604–605; and Edward L. Ayers et al., *American Passages*, brief 4th ed. (Boston: Wadsworth, 2011), 1:355–356. Donations to the Essex Institute were graciously acknowledged in the *Proceedings of the Essex Institute*, and, albeit impressionistically, they seem to me to have diminished during the Panic years.

6. "A Salem Man," "Letter to the Editor," *Boston Daily Advertiser*, August 11, 1858; *Salem Register*, February 11, 1875; "Our Own Historian," "The Story of Leslie's Retreat," *Salem Post*, February 24, 1875; and Henry L. Williams to Dr. Henry Wheaton, February 20, 1875, Peabody Essex Museum.

7. City of Salem, *Memorial Exercises at the Centennial Anniversary of Leslie's Expedition to Salem . . . on Friday February 26, 1875* (Salem, MA, 1875), front matter.

8. "First Centennial of the Revolution," *Salem Register*, March 1, 1875; and L. L. A. Very, "Original Ode," in City of Salem, *Memorial Exercises*, 17.

9. "George B. Loring," in Perry Miller, ed., *The Transcendentalists* (Cambridge, MA: Harvard University Press, 1950), 476. On oratory, Garry Wills, *Lincoln at Gettysburg: The Words that Remade America* (New York: Simon and Schuster, 1992), 48–49.

10. George B. Loring, "Address," in City of Salem, *Memorial Exercises*, 31.

11. Loring, "Address," 32.

12. Loring, "Address," 33, 35, 53–54.

13. Loring, "Address," 55, 56, 72, 58–59.

14. Loring, "Address," 63, 65, 66, 67. On Bancroft and Parkman, Peter Charles Hoffer, *Past Imperfect*, rev. ed. (New York: Public Affairs Press, 2007), 23, 26–27.

15. "Rev. Edmund B. Willson," in *The First Centenary of the North Church and Society in Salem, Massachusetts* (Salem, MA: printed for the Society, 1873), 181–182.

16. Edmund B. Willson, "Address," in City of Salem, *Memorial Exercises*, 88–89, 90.

17. David Blight, *Beyond the Battlefield: Race, Memory and the American Civil War* (Amherst: University of Massachusetts Press, 2002), 60; and David Blight, *Race and Reunion: The Civil War in American Memory* (Cambridge, MA: Harvard University Press, 2001), 2.

18. "The Story," www.northshoreonline.com/dining/plus/leslies/story.htm. Menu items at www.northshoreonline.com/dining/plus/leslies/menu.htm.

19. "HM 64th Regiment of Foot, Major's Company," http://64throf.com.

20. "About PEM," www.pem.org/about/director/. Accessed February 26, 2012.

21. Nathaniel Hawthorne, *The House of the Seven Gables* (Rockville, MD: Arc-Manor, [1851] 2008), 138.

22. Samuel Fowler, "Life and Character of Samuel Parris," *Proceedings of the Essex Institute* 1 (1856), 51, 55; Upham on dreams, ibid., 69; Upham, *Salem Witchcraft*, 1:312, 314, 320, 321.

23. "Leslie's Retreat Trail," www.witchtrail.com/wtctrails.htm#lrt.

EPILOGUE

1. Alfred F. Young and Gregory H. Nobles, "Introduction," in Alfred F. Young and Gregory H. Nobles, eds., *Whose Revolution Was It? Historians Interpret the Founding* (New York: New York University Press, 2011), 8; and Gilbert Ryle, *On the Concept of Mind* (London: Hutchinson, 1949), 16.

2. Pieter Geyl, *Encounters in History* (Gloucester, MA: Peter Smith, [1961] 1977), 97; and David Hackett Fischer, *Paul Revere's Ride* (New York: Oxford University Press, 1994).

3. Alfred Young, *The Shoemaker and the Tea Party* (Boston: Beacon, 1999), 6–7; and Gary B. Nash, *The Unknown American Revolution: The Unruly Birth of Democracy and the Struggle to Create America* (New York: Viking Penguin, 2006), 1.

4. Jack Rakove, *Revolutionaries: A New History of the Invention of America* (New York: Houghton Mifflin Harcourt, 2010), 32.

5. John Adams, quoted in Joseph Ellis, *American Creation: The Triumphs and Tragedies at the Founding of the Republic* (New York: Knopf, 2007), 47; and Bernard Bailyn, *The Ideological Origins of the American Revolution*, rev. ed. (Cambridge, MA: Harvard University Press, 1992), 27, 21.

SUGGESTED FURTHER READING

This section of the book has a somewhat misleading title, because one has to do a little more than read to understand what happened at the North River bridge that cold winter afternoon in 1775. One has to walk the ground, imagining what it was like for the men and officers of the 64th Regiment of Foot and the townspeople of Salem and Marblehead. This is called living history, and, in both senses of the word, enables students of the past to gain a deeper understanding of why men and women of that period thought and acted as they did. One should literally trace their paths in Salem, look for the modern site of Homan's Cove, and figure out how Leslie crossed the South River at the Mill Pond Dam bridge. The books that best accomplish these kinds of living history include David Hackett Fischer's *Paul Revere's Ride* (New York: Oxford University Press, 1994). He has unearthed everything from the name and color of Revere's horse to the number of Gage's men fit, unfit, and wanting (not present) in Boston on April 1, 1775. For my previous efforts in similar cases, see Peter Charles Hoffer, *The Devil's Disciples: The Makers of the Salem Witchcraft Trials* (Baltimore: Johns Hopkins University Press, 1996); *Cry Liberty: The Great Stono River Slave Rebellion of 1739* (New York: Oxford University Press, 2010); and *When Benjamin Franklin Met the Reverend Whitefield: Enlightenment, Revivalism, and the Power of the Printed Word* (Baltimore: Johns Hopkins University Press, 2011).

All of the primary sources I have used for the present account exhibit bias: of patriots and loyalists among the revolutionary actors, and of the glorification of Salem and the Revolution in the nineteenth-century writers' collations. The accounts of Leslie's retreat that survive include only a few contemporary reports, the files of which can be found at the Peabody Essex Museum (PEM) Library; newspaper pieces in the *Salem Gazette* and elsewhere, accessible from the ProQuest Early American Imprints (Series I: Evans, 1639–1800) collection (www.readex.com/readex/product.cfm?product=247); Gage's proclamations and dispatches to Lord Dartmouth, available online at the American Archives website (http://dig.lib.niu.edu/amarch), which is a digital version of the first volumes of Peter Force's *American Archives*; the Gage Papers at the Clements Library, University of Michigan; and local memory contained in memoirs and "as told to" pieces compiled after the fact, appearing at various times in the *Proceedings of the Essex Institute* and the *Essex Institute Historical Collections*. These pieces are cited in the notes.

The disappearance of the raid from secondary sources is striking. On the one hand, the raid was mentioned in every contemporary history of the events leading to independence on both sides of the Atlantic. For example, it appeared in the first volume of William Gordon's *History of the Rise, Progress, and Establishment of the Independence of the United States* (London: Dilly and Buckland, 1788); Charles Stedman's *History of the Origin, Progress, and Termination of the American War* (Dublin, 1794); and Abiel Holmes's *American Annals* (Cambridge, MA: Hilliard, 1805). But by its centennial, the raid had become a story of local interest only. Charles Moses Endicott was the most truthworthy of the latter set of authors, for he was able to question the last generation of Salem men and women who knew someone who was alive in 1775. George B. Loring and Edmund L. Willson added material to Endicott's piece (without giving any source for their additions). Next, Robert S. Rantoul "knew" what Loring and Willson did not. As new evidence comes to light, historians will revise existing accounts, as Ellen Chase did in her account in the second volume of *The Beginnings of the American Revolution* (New York: Baker and Taylor, 1910)—based on a new biography of Paul Revere—but Loring, Willson, and Rantoul, as was common in the historical literature of their period, simply filled in details they thought should have been there.

There is less on the Salem gunpowder raid than one might hope for in the modern secondary literature. The foremost twentieth-century historian of colonial Salem was James Duncan Phillips. Better known today for the chair named in his honor at Harvard University and the library named after him at the PEM, his *Salem in the Seventeenth Century* (Boston: Houghton Mifflin, 1933) and *Salem in the Eighteenth Century* (Boston: Houghton Mifflin, 1937) are still immensely readable. In the latter volume he dedicated one short chapter to the raid, which concluded: "If Great Britain was willing to admit before the nineteenth of April that the Revolution had begun in Salem, there seems no good reason why Americans should deny it, and perhaps our patriotic friends in Lexington and Concord might bear this in mind" (360). With the exception of the fine U.S. National Park Service's Handbook 126, *Salem: Maritime Salem in the Age of Sail* (Salem, MA: Peabody Essex Museum, 2009), and Fischer's *Paul Revere's Ride*, Phillips's plea has gone unanswered. As one local newspaper report, claiming to have examined all the facts, concluded seventy years after Phillips's book was published, the raid "remains a sort of local legend or myth with much fuzziness and multiple mysteries" (John Goff, "More to the Story: Col. Alexander Leslie's Retreat," Gatehouse News Service, February 9, 2008, www.wickedlocal .com/salem/news/lifestyle/columnists/x288025073#axzz1mO5nv6Yf/).

Excellent modern, voluminous surveys of the coming of the Revolution, like Merrill Jensen's 750-plus page *The Founding of a Nation: A History of the American Revolution 1763–1776* (New York: Oxford University Press, 1968), cover the events in Salem that led to the Massachusetts Provincial Congress, but then move on to other venues. Robert Middlekauf's award-winning *The Glorious Cause: The American Revolution, 1763–1789*, revised edition (New York: Oxford University Press, 2005), quotes Pickering's manual for militias, but has nothing to say about Pickering's role in the Salem gunpowder raid, and mentions Alexander Leslie—when he was a general. Textbooks seem to skip directly from the meeting of the First Continental Congress to Lexington and Concord, as does "The Coming of the American Revolution" website at the Massachusetts Historical Society (http://masshist.org/revolution/topics .php). The Wikipedia site on the history of Salem (http://en.wikipedia.org/wiki/ Salem,_Massachusetts/) does include a paragraph on the raid. Though I had spent a good deal of time working in Salem and at nearby archives for two books on the witchcraft trials and another on the sensory experience of witchcraft, I was unaware of the Salem raid until I read the six pages (58–64) that David Hackett Fischer devoted to it in *Paul Revere's Ride*. Indeed, that may be the reason why the pages above owe so much to Fischer's research and quarrel so often with his conclusions.

A broader perspective can put the many fragmentary and elusive accounts into a usable framework. That framework will include questions like, "who was running things in Salem—the common folk or the men of affairs?" Some historians see the Revolution as a top-down affair, while others see it as rising from the bottom up. The gap between these schools grows wider with each of their respective publications. As uncompromising toward one another's views as the Whigs and Tories were before the final breach with Britain, leading scholars' accounts leave the reader wondering what really happened. If only one could see the events of the Revolution for oneself. A sampling of works considering the Revolution from the top down: Bernard Bailyn, *Ideological Origins of the American Revolution*, rev. ed. (Cambridge, MA: Harvard University Press, 1992); Jack Rakove, *Revolutionaries: A New History of the Invention of America* (New York: Houghton Mifflin, 2010); and Gordon Wood, *The Radicalism of the American Revolution* (New York: Knopf, 1991). And of those looking at the Revolution from the bottom up: T. H. Breen, *American Insurgents, American Patriots: The Revolution of the People* (New York: Hill and Wang, 2010); Edward Countryman, *The American Revolution*, revised edition (New York: Hill and Wang, 2003); and Gary Nash, *The Unknown American Revolution: The Unruly Birth of Democracy and the Struggle to Create America* (New York: Viking Penguin, 2006). None of these histories spend much time in Salem on February 26, 1775, but if one accepts the top-down thesis, then the key actors are Leslie, Mason, Pickering, and that lot. If one rejects the top-down approach, then it is the distillery boys and the sailors on the chains holding the drawbridge up, and the farmers who hid the cannons, who form the real story, because in their acts they declared their independence not only from the British Empire, but also from their "betters."

INDEX